HEALING

HERBAL

SOUPS

HEALING
HERBAL
SOUPS

BOOST YOUR IMMUNITY *and* WEATHER *the* SEASONS *with* TRADITIONAL CHINESE RECIPES

ROSE CHEUNG
and GENEVIEVE WONG

TILLER PRESS

New York   London   Toronto   Sydney   New Delhi

An Imprint of Simon & Schuster, Inc.
1230 Avenue of the Americas
New York, NY 10020

First Tiller Press trade paperback edition September 2021

TILLER PRESS and colophon are registered trademarks of Simon & Schuster, Inc.

For information about special discounts for bulk purchases, please contact
Simon & Schuster Special Sales at 1-866-506-1949 or business@simonandschuster.com.

The Simon & Schuster Speakers Bureau can bring authors to your live event.
For more information or to book an event, contact the Simon & Schuster Speakers Bureau
at 1-866-248-3049 or visit our website at www.simonspeakers.com.

Interior design by Jennifer Chung
Photography by Dylan + Jeni

Manufactured in China

3 5 7 9 10 8 6 4

Library of Congress Cataloging-in-Publication Data

Names: Wong, Genevieve, author. | Cheung, Rose, author.
Title: Healing herbal soups : boost your immunity and weather the seasons with traditional
Chinese recipes / by Genevieve Wong and Rose Cheung. Description: New York : Tiller Press, 2021. |
Includes index. Identifiers: LCCN 2021005807 (print) | LCCN 2021005808 (ebook) |
ISBN 9781982176112 (paperback) | ISBN 9781982176129 (ebook) Subjects: LCSH: Soups. |
Cooking (Herbs) | Medicine, Chinese. | Classification: LCC TX757 .W66 2021 (print) |
LCC TX757 (ebook) | DDC 641.81/3—dc23

LC record available at https://lccn.loc.gov/2021005807
LC ebook record available at https://lccn.loc.gov/2021005808

ISBN 978-1-9821-7611-2
ISBN 978-1-9821-7612-9 (ebook)

To Beatrice, Chris, Theresa, and Jennifer:
Thank you for weathering the seasons with us.
We will forever be in debt to you for your love and support.

CONTENTS

Chinese herbal pharmacy Wing Hop Fung in Southern California.

PART I

INTRODUCTION to CHINESE HERBAL SOUPS

The universe creates life on this Earth. It also crafts an unimaginable support system for everything that we see, feel, and touch.

Unfortunately, as we humans increase in wisdom and technological advances, we have lost touch with the natural way of eating. We no longer understand how to cure ourselves of sickness by consuming the right plants, flowers, and herbs that surround us. The primitive idea of eating for survival has been replaced with a completely different concept of eating for pleasure and taste.

Scientific advances in medicine and technology have made us forget about the old and the traditional. Our modern lifestyle creates stress, fatigue, pollution, and the world of preservatives in our food. Together these bring on illnesses that we either ignore or try to fix through medicines that alleviate symptoms but do little to cure the underlying cause.

Southern Chinese (the Cantonese) believe that health can be maintained by drinking herbal soups, that is, mixing herbs with meat and vegetables in order to create healing broths to weather the seasons. This is commonly referred to as the Nurturing Life with Soup concept. The fact that the Chinese population has not only survived but flourished is great evidence that their health maintenance system through diet works—or at least *something* they do is right.

The practice of making herbal soups is a tradition that extends far beyond China. Recipes have been adopted and adapted throughout the Orient and Southeast Asia in Japan, Korea, and Singapore, among others.

Note that herbal soups are not the same as the medicinal decoctions prescribed by Traditional Chinese Medicine practitioners. These are formulas you can obtain after a personal consultation with a Chinese herbalist, and they are personalized for each person's illness and constitution, so only that person should be drinking the herbs. In Cantonese, we jokingly refer to these concentrated liquids as "bitter herbs" because they are usually blackish, harsh tasting, and pungent, and for those who are very sick, the decoction might even have a muddy consistency.

In contrast, Chinese herbal soups are a much more pleasurable experience. They are translucent broths that are easy to drink and work as natural remedies for common ailments. Once you consume one, you should immediately feel a healing, peaceful effect.

ROSE'S STORY

I grew up in Hong Kong with four sisters. My mother and grandmother cooked all kinds of herbal soups as part of our daily diet. It didn't matter if we had a cold from playing in the rain or a stomachache from eating too many oily, greasy foods during Chinese New Year. My mother and my grandmother always knew which soups to make to clear out our blocked systems and bring them back to health.

Traditional Chinese medicine (TCM), also referred to as Oriental medicine, is one of my great passions. TCM is a medical system that dates back to the third century BCE and is designed to prevent, diagnose, and treat disease through herbal medicine and therapies like acupuncture and moxibustion (a type of heat therapy).

I have seen how Western medicine fails to cure certain illnesses and sicknesses. Over twenty years ago, my mother was diagnosed with lymphoma, and the oncologist told her she had only three years to live. We ended up getting a second opinion from a Chinese herbalist. Thanks to the herbal formulas he prescribed for my mom, she lived another thirteen years before she passed away.

TCM isn't just for chronic diseases. Many of my American colleagues and friends suffer from small illnesses like cold sores, upset stomach, or dry lips and are not aware that they can help themselves by eating the right mixture of food with some herbs.

When my eldest daughter, Genevieve, went to college in New York City, I told her what to do when she came down with a cold, a sore throat, and canker sores. Having grown up in Los Angeles, she was not used to living in an environment with four seasons, and her body had issues adjusting, so I advised her on what types of soups she should drink to improve her condition. To my surprise, she listened. It was funny for me to hear how she went to Chinatown to buy herbs, quoting what I often said to her in daily life: "I need to buy LoHan Guo [monk fruit] to get rid of my congestion." After all, she is an ABC (American-born Chinese).

One day while we were chatting on the phone about how to boil these herbs to drink, she asked me a simple question: "Mom, what do Gwai Lo [people who are not Chinese] do when they get a sore throat or feel heated up in their bodies?" I paused and responded, "They just have to suffer through it and get well themselves." Her question stuck in my mind for years. Yes, what do people who don't know about TCM do? They deserve to learn what we know. It's not that hard.

As I got older, my Chinese friends started complaining to me that they didn't feel well. They were having issues with their bodies because of this or that. I started offering advice about what herbs to cook in their soup and what to eat in order to help lessen their problems and accelerate their recovery. Gradually over the years, I received calls and emails from more and more of my friends requesting similar advice.

I offered suggestions, but I had to tell them repeatedly that I was not their doctor. I have no medical training, just old world recipes and knowledge passed down to me from the women in my family. But what I said did not matter to them. Recently, the requests from families and friends have changed into "I think you should write down all these soups for us to refer to instead of having us call you" or "Maybe you should write a book teaching all of us about what soups to boil and when."

One day I was lecturing my youngest daughter, Henrietta, about her not knowing what to eat when she came down with a slight cold. She talked back and said: "You should have written all this in English for me!" *How ungrateful*, I thought. Within days, Henrietta presented me with herbal soup forms that she had made on her laptop, with sections like soup name, purpose, and ingredients to fill in. I thought this was a ridiculous demand. But then I started thinking that maybe I *should* write down my recipes, not only for her but for all of my friends. I am fortunate enough to possess all of this knowledge, and I should put it in writing to help others.

Genevieve agreed that it would be a worthwhile undertaking. A TV producer and writer, she helped me do additional research in order to put a book proposal together. (An amusing note: Genevieve once told me that she liked the idea of doing a soup cookbook because unlike cooking, boiling soup didn't require much know-how! "It is accessible to people regardless of their race, sex, ethnicity, relationship status, and skill set," she once told me. "That never happens, not even in primetime television.")

One thing Genevieve and I both want to communicate in this cookbook is that we understand that not everyone is familiar with Chinese herbs and how they can help boost good health. Not everyone has the knowledge to nurture life through soup. We also recognize that it is important to incorporate certain herbs into the soups to make them attractive and delicious enough for as many people as possible to drink and reap their benefits. Teaching people to use natural medicines instead of turning to pills will be a slow education process that will bring all of us closer to Mother Nature, who has provided us with remedies we used to know about but have now, sadly, forgotten.

INTRODUCING *the* SEASONS *and* HERBS

This book reintroduces (or introduces) you to all the flowers, roots, and herbs we should be eating and the art of blending them into soup. We discuss how each season brings different challenges to our bodies and advise you on what you should eat in order to help defend against and cope with changing weather. We believe that if you can stabilize your body through these temperature fluctuations, your immune system will be better prepared to protect against sicknesses like colds and flus that come on when you feel the most run down. Contrary to popular belief, you cannot go around taking herbs at random or pairing them up with others without knowing about their side effects. That is very dangerous. Because herbs are made up of chemicals in natural form, no one should combine them without professional guidance. The combinations we came up with are purposely broad and simple for that reason.

Spring is the season when cold changes to warm, with moments of cold and then warmth within this change. Our emotions begin to churn with the weather, a fluctuation that causes uneasiness and discomfort in our bodies. This is the best time to clear out your liver and pancreas of toxins that have accumulated over the winter. It is an even better time to consume flower teas and eat herbs that are good for your spleen and stomach, such as Chinese yam, lotus seeds, and makhana. Avoid sour foods like lemons.

Summer is hot and humid. (In Southern California where we reside, it is dry.) This is a good time to eat melons, such as watermelons and winter melons, because they expel the heat trapped inside our bodies. It is also best to cook kudzu root and adzuki beans because they help to drive away the dampness trapped within the heat.

In fall, the weather changes from warm to slightly cold and dry. Our skin feels dehydrated, and the parched air can affect our lungs. To soothe this dryness, sand ginseng, polygonatum, Asian pears, and snow fungus can conserve moisture in our organs.

Winter's chill affects our bodies in a different way than fall does. In this season, it is important to consume meat, such as goat and fish, and glutinous rice because they help conserve heat in our body. It is also a good time for walnuts, black beans, and chestnuts. But avoid spicy food and large amounts of ginger and garlic.

If this is your first time hearing terms like *snow fungus* and *Chinese yam*, do not be concerned. They will become a part of your regular vocabulary once you read this book, and we will help you learn what they are and how to cook with them.

Locating the right herbs for purchase may be a small challenge for novices, and we will tell you how to do this. Our hope is that after working on a few recipes, you will realize that herbal soups are a simple process and you will love what you have discovered. The upside is that boiling soups with herbs doesn't require as many skills as cooking them. We have assembled some easy soup recipes with simple herbs and others that are more advanced. You should pick the ones you feel are easier to start with and then gradually move on to try the more complicated recipes.

One of our long-term goals is to sell assembled packages of soup ingredients for you, and they are available on our website for this book: www.healingherbalsoups.com. We will also sell Chinese soup-making cookware with timers and auto functions. We understand that not everyone lives close to a Chinatown or has access to a Chinese herbal pharmacy.

It's time to see nature's remedies and to revive knowledge that has long been forgotten or ignored. We hope our cookbook can educate more people about Chinese herbs through a delicious and enjoyable adventure of soups.

Start the year right by getting healthier and feeling better—and congratulations on this new gift of life purchase!

GENEVIEVE'S STORY

Every body is different. Mine, for example, is a slim Asian American woman's: I am 5'3" and around 115 pounds. I am curvy in some places and petite in others. While I am known in some social circles for having a strong personality, I have never been considered mighty, at least not when it came to my health.

I was born with eczema, a condition that makes the skin red and itchy. For as long as I can remember, I had rashes that flared up in the middle of my arms and behind my knees. Both my mother and grandmother suffered from the disease, and all my Western doctors told me that what I had was genetic.

I was never in pain from my eczema or too inconvenienced, although having it was always at the back of my mind, even at a very young age. According to my mother, the first words I ever spoke in Chinese were, "I'm itchy."

Throughout my childhood, dermatologists prescribed hydrocortisone creams and ointments that would calm my flare-ups, but relief never lasted. Just after I healed from my rashes, they returned. It was a never-ending cycle with a long list of alleged culprits: seafood, pollution, wheat, strawberries, and others.

Like most other people who suffer from eczema, I was prone to allergies. Cats and pollen triggered intense sneezing and watery eyes. And of course they brought on more rashes. At school, kids would ask me about my scaly patches, but instead of alienating me, they were actually quite sympathetic. The nice thing about my eczema (yes, there was an upside) was that it didn't stop me from living my life. I could still go anywhere I wanted, see the places and people I needed to see, and eat and do the things I pleased.

That was not the case with asthma, a lung condition I developed when I was thirteen years old. I was living a carefree existence at the time, going to school and behaving like any other teenager. However, if you ask my mom what I was up to, she'd probably tell you that I was going through a rebellious stage. I disobeyed her constantly: skipping out on her home-cooked meals and herbal broths to eat at McDonald's, using the proceeds from my lemonade stand to buy junk food behind her back, staying up late watching MTV, and running around wearing skimpy clothes no matter how cold it was, preferring to be fashionable instead.

Of course, that's not how I remember things. What I do recall is that I was going through a lot of hormonal changes when I was twelve and thirteen, and my body responded differently once I became a woman. Suddenly I became inflamed and bloated easily. My allergies and eczema worsened. Rashes began appearing on parts of my body where they hadn't been before. My immune system seemed to have fewer strong days, which meant I was getting coughs and colds much more frequently. Whenever I came in contact with allergens for prolonged periods of time, I sneezed so much that I was exhausted and had to take a nap to function normally again.

The turning point came when I got sick with three coughs in a row. No matter how many antibiotics I took, I could not shake off the illness. During the last bout, my condition took a turn for the worse: I developed bronchitis. Suddenly I wasn't just coughing; I was wheezing. My lungs felt as if they were filled with water, and I hacked nonstop until I was red in the face. My chest hurt, and I had to sleep with two pillows in order to breathe.

Over six months, my health got even worse. Minor breathlessness devolved into episodes of fighting for air. I felt as if I was being suffocated for hours on end, and on some days, I felt like I was drowning. I couldn't run, I could barely study, and it no longer felt comfortable to talk for too long.

I don't know how I went to school. I don't know how I survived. Every minute was harrowing.

Each time it became too unbearable, I returned to my pediatrician, a Western doctor, for answers. One day, he gave me the bad news: I had come down with bronchitis so many times that I had developed asthma. It's a chronic disease in which the airways narrow and swell with mucus, which could make breathing difficult and trigger coughing. There was no cure for this, but there was a way that I could breathe better: the doctor wrote me a prescription for a steroid inhaler.

"This will help you breathe instantly," he assured me and sent me off on my merry way.

"Thank you," I said on my way out, convinced that I would go back to normal within months. I figured that once I was able to breathe, everything would fall back into place.

Boy, was I wrong. Although the inhaler did help me to breathe in that moment and in the days that followed, what I didn't know was that there wasn't ever going to be a solution to my problem, at least not in Western medicine. I was now saddled with another health issue on top of my eczema.

Initially I used my inhaler whenever I had a cough or a cold, which was when my asthmatic symptoms really flared. However, by the end of high school, I was using the inhaler every day—even when I wasn't sick.

My mom tried to help, but she didn't have any personal experience with breathing issues. However, she did know of an herbalist who operated out of an herbal pharmacy next door to my dad's office.

When I went to see the herbalist with my mother, he prescribed me a long list of herbs to boil at home. I drank the dark liquids twice a day for two weeks. They tasted awful, but when I finished the herbs, I did feel better. Most important, I noticed a decrease in the number of times I used my inhaler. Unfortunately, the medicine failed to take away the "wet" feeling I had in my lungs, which by this time felt clogged and dirty.

I never went back to see the doctor again. Instead, I exercised more. With my lungs feeling slightly stronger, I began running. I started my workouts with slow jogs around the block and gradually built up to running around the block for twenty minutes. It was hard at first because I had to stop and restart dozens of times. On the runs, I coughed up a lot of the mucus I felt had been trapped inside my lungs and sweated out many of the toxins.

I lost weight and felt much better within a matter of months. I weaned myself off my inhaler, using it only when I was sick. *Was that it?* I'd ask myself. *I just needed to exercise more? I wonder why nobody told me this.* But this was not going to be the end of my health journey.

After high school, I went to college in New York City and later Chicago, which really did a number on my body. Coming from Southern California, I was not used to having four seasons. I did not know that each time the weather changed, I'd feel it in my lungs. In fact, my daily asthma attacks returned. On some days, I felt that I was

❀   **Healing Herbal Soups**

drowning, and on other days being choked. Sometimes I felt the both were happening at once.

Exercise, eating clean, and drinking more water were no longer enough. I begrudgingly returned to using my inhaler, stopped exercising, and gained weight. My immune system went down again—all the hard work I spent getting better went down the drain.

I don't know how I went to school. I don't know how I survived. Every minute was harrowing.

On my twenty-fourth birthday, I was tasked with blowing out the candles on the cake my friends had gotten me. As joyful as the occasion was, I was hiding an embarrassing secret: for the first time in my life, my lungs were too weak to blow the candles out. Thanks to some good acting classes in college, I enlisted my little sister to help, and it went without a hitch. But it was a sad, depressing moment for me.

EMBRACING HERBALISM

When I graduated from graduate school, I headed back to Los Angeles. My mother sent me to an herbalist named Dr. Zhang in the San Gabriel Valley. He had helped my mother through menopause, and she was convinced that he could help me with my asthma.

After examining me and taking my pulse, Dr. Zhang gave me a prescription of herbs that he altered every other week when I went to see him. He also explained that he would try to cure me, but ten years of damage on my lungs was not going to go away within a month or two of treatment. It could be years. (This is why taking early action is important.)

I nodded and repeatedly said that I didn't want to be a slave to my disease anymore and I was willing to try anything. Within one month of drinking Dr. Zhang's herbs, I stopped getting eczema. A few more years passed. and I could feel my lungs drying out. Instead of having colds and coughs five times a year, I had them two or three times a year, like most other people. My inflammation went down, and I lost weight. I no longer had to sleep on two pillows. Every year, my breathing got better. I could run longer distances. I could go camping without my body freaking out. It was okay to visit friends who had cats.

After not leading a normal life for over a decade, I was given a second chance at life. I could even accomplish some goals I had on my bucket list without fear that I would be too sick or weak to do them.

Once my lungs stabilized and I brought down my frequency of asthma attacks to once a year (always when summer dipped into fall), I realized I needed to do all that I could to maintain the improved health I had. In addition to drinking my herbs, I made a vow to never touch drugs or alcohol or sign up to do death-defying activities. I continued to drink my bitter herbs diligently twice a day.

Finally, when I turned thirty, Dr. Zhang told me that I didn't need to see him as much. I could cut down on drinking his medicine and imbibe only when I was under the weather. In the meantime, he advised me to maintain my health by eating clean, and to see him whenever the seasons changed. My lungs would be the most sensitive then.

Most important, Dr. Zhang gave me suggestions on what to eat in order to maintain good health. Starting with a diet that was free of dairy and refined sugar, he then prescribed a weekly soup. Nine times out of ten he instructed me to boil a soup with a specific kind of meat, vegetables, and one or two Chinese herbs. He also told me why the liquids were effective, most often because there were herbs in the recipes that decreased the mucus in my lungs. Intrigued, I began studying recipes online on my own and started comparing them to the ones my mom had compiled in her notebook.

I promised myself that once I healed, I would use the knowledge that Dr. Zhang gave me to try to spread awareness about the power of TCM.

So here we are. If you're reading this book, you're probably looking to improve your health. You're in the right place. You don't need to be a culinary genius to boil herbal soups, just some recipes and a commitment to some consistency. These broths are not a cure-all. You still need to maintain a healthy lifestyle. If you're already sick, drinking the liquids may help accelerate your recovery.

FINAL NOTES *and* POINTERS

Keep in mind that the soups Dr. Zhang recommended for me were more on the medicinal side. If you consume them, chances are that you will have a very strong reaction. As I learned, there are other recipes that are more generic and have less potent ingredients. These are the kinds of broths that my mother and I share with you in this book.

Because we are not medical professionals, we enlisted Dr. Eddie Chui, a preeminent TCM doctor, researcher, and professor, to vet the recipes before we translated them from Chinese into English.

Finally, remember that *under no circumstances* should you be mixing and matching herbs! Leave the combinations that we suggest alone.

We are all living busy lives, but that doesn't mean you don't have time to make a healing broth for yourself. Remember that you deserve this, and if you don't have time to watch a pot on a stove, you can always use an automatic soup cooker: pour in all the ingredients, set a timer, press the On button, and the broth will be ready when you come home from work.

We hope that the information and stories we have shared with you are useful and enough to get you motivated. May the solace that Chinese herbs have brought me and our family travel to you.

1

TRADITIONAL CHINESE MEDICINE

You are probably familiar with acupuncture: a form of treatment that involves inserting thin needles through a person's skin at specific points on the body. Perhaps you've even heard about cupping, a practice that places cups on the skin to create suction. Maybe you've seen groups of seniors practicing the martial art of tai chi in the park in order to improve their energy and circulation.

Is that all that Traditional Chinese Medicine is about? Obviously not, as we have already discussed other aspects of TCM in the Introduction. Nonetheless, it has always made us chuckle that such a small portion of TCM has garnered so much attention and representation in today's modern world. Traditional Chinese Medicine has been around for more than two millennia and is so much more than acupuncture, cupping, and tai chi.

Traditional Chinese Medicine is most widely practiced in the Sino sphere—that is, countries that are heavily influenced by Chinese culture. The roots of TCM lie in the doctrines of two ancient medical texts: *Huangdi Nei Jing* (*The Yellow Emperor's Inner Canon*), which was compiled during the Warring States period of 475 to 221 BC, and *Shang Han Lun* (*The Treatise on Cold Damage Disorders and Miscellaneous Illnesses*), which was written at the end of the Eastern Han dynasty between 200 and 205 AD. In the ancient days, doctors tried out herbs on themselves (they had no animal testing or laboratories to conduct research in) and wrote the results down in these books that were handed down for generations.

True TCM is opposed to the use of "medicine" to cure diseases. Instead, the theory and practice focus on restoring order in the human body by opening the lock that suppresses immunity. It then allows one's immune system to cure the disease by itself. Unlike Western medicine, TCM believes it is the human body, not medication, that has the power to heal the wound.

TCM practitioners start by restoring the body to normal through herbal therapies—ones that mostly use flowers, roots, stems, tree bark, and so on. Instead of extracting ingredients from herbs like Western medicine does, TCM uses herbs in their original, unprocessed, or specially processed form. Often the plants are dried and then cooked later, although sometimes fresh herbs are used. The belief is that ingredients in their natural form are easier for the body to absorb and more effective than in their extracted form, because every herb has many nutrients.

Like Western medicine, TCM perceives the human body in many ways, but TCM has supplemental theories. According to TCM, the human body has different pressure points where the nervous system and the organs are interrelated and connected. The points are called acupoints, which are connected by *meridians*. It is a distribution system that carries and distributes *qi* through the blood. Qi (pronounced "chi") is the energy flow that people are born with, and it determines the individual's healthiness. If there is a blockage at a qi point, practitioners can trace it to where the flow is disrupted and determine which organ is having problems.

A TCM diagnosis begins with a full evaluation of a patient's blood-flow pattern, breathing pattern, qi, and pulse. The herbalist most likely starts the session by examining your pulse: you extend your arm and the doctor puts three fingers on your wrist and begins "listening." Next, your blood-flow pattern will be taken, and your tongue, which reveals the condition of certain organs, is examined. Practitioners also pay close attention to the symptoms displayed on your face and by your smell.

Once the diagnosis is complete, herbal medicine is prescribed. The doctor comes up with a formula custom-made for you and made up of many herbs. TCM practitioners consider these formulas to be proprietary and guard them closely.

The art of the prescription lies in how the herbalist mixes and matches the herbs. Let's say a doctor wants to use herb A, but it has some side effects. He can add herb B to the mix to completely disable or neutralize the unwanted effects of herb A. Or he may select other herbs to optimize the results of herb A.

The herbal formula is 90 percent of what TCM is about. Therapies like acupuncture and cupping are instituted in order to enhance the recovery of the patient. There are other techniques, too, that are used just as often—for example, heat application, moxibustion, bone setting, qi therapy, scratching and scraping of meridians, massaging special pressure points, and applying external patches, all of which are effective but not as widely known. The purpose of these techniques is to complement the herbal medicine.

Note that the most popular technique from the list, acupuncture, can relieve symptoms for around forty-eight hours; it cannot cure health conditions permanently. It's therefore only a temporary fix, although it can be lasting in some cases. The Chinese concept of maintaining health is to eat right, drink nurturing soups, and exercise well. Herbal prescriptions are always the last resort. Exercise covers not only our muscles but our organs. The key to good maintenance is to keep healthy patterns of sleep, rest, work, play, exercise, diet, and lifestyle. When the seasons change, we need to be more vigilant about keeping our body strong. This might include boiling more soups to prepare for external changes in the environment and keeping your lifestyle healthy.

This book follows the same philosophies of TCM. We teach you how to strengthen your immune system in order to fight illness and disease and instruct you on how to develop an overall healthy lifestyle to support your immune system with a clean diet, appropriate exercise, and a good amount of rest. In order to do that, we need you to understand your body type, as well as the yin and yang concept and how it works, so that you can better select the right food and nutrients for your body.

WHICH BODY TYPE ARE YOU?

Traditional Chinese Medicine believes that people can be classified into three main body types: cold, hot, or neutral, terms that refer to one's body constitution and are not a direct reference to the individual's body temperature. Knowing your body type will help you understand what your body is susceptible to and how it responds to illness.

Most of us are born with either a cold or a hot body. Very few people are born neutral, which means that their body constitution is 100 percent balanced and perfect.

A typical cold person has the following characteristics:

- Hands and feet that are always cold
- Slightly pale and light complexion
- Does not like cold temperatures
- Prefers warm drinks
- Has pain in certain parts of the body at times and the pain increases with a drastic weather change
- Watery stool

Those with a cold body type will feel colder than most other people during winter and less hot in the summer.

In general, women skew on the colder side because women's bodies have to do so much work to go through menstruation, pregnancy, childbirth, and menopause. We are physically weaker than men because our bodies go through so many hormonal changes.

A typical hot person has the following characteristics:

- Body that always feels warm or hot
- Eyes that feel dry and are slightly red
- A constant desire for cold drinks
- Slightly dry mouth and lips
- Slightly red complexion
- Urine that is usually quite yellow and limited in quantity
- Stool that is usually harder and slightly dry, with some suffering frequent constipation
- Gets cold sores easily and frequently

Those with a hot body type will feel hotter than most people during summer and less cold in the winter. On the surface, hot bodies appear healthier than cold bodies because they have fewer reactions to food, even when they eat the wrong things. Hot body types often have higher-than-average blood pressure.

No matter what body type you are, it is still important to be prepared before every season arrives so that your body can adjust to changes more easily easier and efficiently. That is why you should aim to eat foods that complement what your body needs.

FOOD ENERGIES

Like body types, food is also categorized into different energies: they can have hot, cold, warm, cool, or neutral properties. Again, these words refer to the energies of food, not the actual temperatures at which they are served.

A cold body type should avoid cold food because it will make the body colder. A hot body type should avoid hot food because it will make the body hotter. Warm food is between hot and neutral, and cool food is between cold and neutral. Neutral is neither hot nor cold, which means everyone can eat this type of food.

The idea is to neutralize the body and not to aggravate its tendency toward its existing deficiency. Thus if you have a cold body, you should try to eat more hot or warm food so that your body will not get colder, but warmer.

Don't be extreme and abstain from all foods that aren't right for your energy. Just eat less of that kind of food. As long as we balance intake well, cold bodies can take in a limited amount of cold food and hot bodies can take in a limited amount of hot food.

Here are some common foods and their categories:

	COLD FOOD	COOL FOOD
VEGETABLES	Bamboo shoots	Asparagus
	Bitter melon	Bean sprouts from soybeans
	Kombu (sea algae)	Bok choy
	Lettuce	Celery
	Mustard greens	Cucumbers
	Mung bean sprouts	Eggplant
	Napa cabbage	Green peppers
	Seaweed (nori)	Spinach
	Turnips	Tofu
	Wheatgrass	Tomatoes
MEAT AND SEAFOOD	Clams	Duck
	Mussels	Rabbit
	Shellfish	
	Snails	
FRUIT	Banana	Coconut
	Cantaloupe	Durian
	Grapefruit	Figs
	Honeydew	Guava
	Mangosteen	Longan
	Persimmon	Mango
	Watermelon	Mulberries
		Olives
		Orange
		Pears
		Watermelon
OTHER	Ice cream	Chrysanthemum
	Green tea	Honeysuckle flowers
	White tea	Lily leaf
		Mint
		Red tea
		Rock sugar
		Soy milk

	HOT FOOD	WARM FOOD
VEGETABLES	Black pepper Chile peppers Jalapeno peppers Garlic Ginger	Chestnuts Garlic shoots Onion Parsley
MEAT	Lamb Mutton Venison	Beef Chicken Pigeon
FRUIT	Durian Lychee	Cherries Nectarines Peaches Pineapple Plums
OTHER	Anise Chocolate Coffee Curry	Almonds Pistachios Walnuts

	NEUTRAL FOOD
VEGETABLES	Broccoli Carrots Chinese cabbage Chinese yams String beans Potatoes Pumpkin Yams
MEAT	Fish Pork
FRUIT	Apples Grapes Lemon Papaya
OTHER	Black beans Black rice Corn Eggs Milk Red beans Rice Wheat

CHAPTER

2

The **THREE MAIN CAUSES** *of* **ILLNESS**

YIN *and* YANG IMBALANCES

Today, we often toss around the words *yin* and *yang* to describe two people who are complementary opposites. In TCM, those words are used to classify the body's energies, organs, and deficiencies. For example, the heart, liver, spleen, lungs, and kidneys are yin organs. The intestines (small and large), bladder, gallbladder, stomach, and triple energizer are yang organs. Yang organs digest food and transport the nutrients to the yin organs. The yin organs secrete necessary fluids and hormones to nourish the yang organs for smoother metabolism.

The term *triple energizer* or *triple warmer* refers to the energetic pathways that traverse the upper, middle, and lower cavities of the body. Its main job is to monitor qi and fluids that surround the internal organs.

Yang makes things happen, while yin provides the material necessary for the actions to occur. This interdependence makes them inseparable. Except for a few lucky individuals, most people suffer from either a yin or a yang imbalance. There is no way around this: women in particular are usually more yin deficient than men.

While the theory of yin and yang has origins in Taoism and has taken on a more mystical definition in Western culture in recent years, we will be dealing with the duality in more practical terms.

Here is some guidance on how to know if you are yin or yang deficient:

SYMPTOMS OF PEOPLE WHO LACK YIN

1. Center of hands, feet, and chest feel hot
2. Thirsty and dry in the mouth
3. Preference for cold drinks
4. Red, moist complexion
5. Slight insomnia
6. Vivid dreams
7. Constipation
8. Darker-color urine
9. Occasional pain during urination
10. Narrow, red tongue
11. Sweats during sleep

SYMPTOMS OF PEOPLE WHO LACK YANG

1. Hands and feet that feel cold
2. Preference for hot drinks

3. Waist and ankles that feel slightly cramped and weak
4. Thinning hair
5. Watery stool
6. Long urination and clear urine
7. Lack of energy all day
8. Always sleepy
9. Slightly pale lips

Both cold and hot body types can suffer from yin and yang energy deficiencies, and some may even be deficient in both.

If you believe you lack yin energy, try to eat food that is "moisturizing" and slightly "cool." Pears, honey, tofu, sesame, and lily bulbs are good foods that can ameliorate this condition. Drink six to eight cups of water every day, but make sure that it is not cold water, which disperses your energy. (That is why TCM discourages people from drinking cold water in general.) Sea cucumber, abalone, and snow fungus are strongest in the production of yin qi.

Individuals who lack yang energy should try to eat food that is "warm" to boost their levels. Beef, lamb, and chicken are hot foods that will help produce yang energy. Examples of warm foods are peppers, mutton, ginger, dried longan, and chives. Do not drink cold drinks or green tea.

A yang deficiency can create serious issues for the body and can lead to obesity, internal secretion imbalance, kidney problems, fertility issues, and even cancer. Here are some practices in your daily life that will help you spruce up your yang energy:

1. Take short afternoon naps.
2. Get sunlight for 20 minutes (especially in the morning before 10:00 a.m.). Make sure to get sun on your back.
3. Go to a sauna.
4. Soak in hot springs.
5. Protect your head, back, and stomach from the cold.
6. Keep your ankles warm.
7. Interact more socially.
8. Eat more food of a warm or hot nature.

Now that you know how to build up your yang qi, here is a guide for what *not* to do! These five bad practices will dissipate yang energy:

1. **DO NOT WEAR SHOES OR SOCKS THAT LEAVE YOUR ANKLES EXPOSED.**
   An important acupoint at the ankle can leak yang energy, so be sure to cover your ankles.
2. **AVOID GARMENTS THAT EXPOSE THE WAIST AND BELLY BUTTON.**
   Although it may be sexy to wear clothing like this, it exposes two acupoints:

one on the back of the waist and the other connected to the kidneys. The belly button itself is also an acupoint that's connected to the tummy and kidneys. Thus, exposing these points to cold temperatures and external elements may lead to poor circulation and pain in the lower half of your body.

3. DO NOT WASH YOUR HAIR AND BODY EARLY IN THE MORNING, RIGHT AFTER YOU WAKE UP. Your body's energy rises with the sun and the Earth, so at sunrise, your body's yang qi begins to grow and develop; by midday, your yang energy reaches its height and gradually slows down as the sun sets. Therefore, washing your hair early in the morning is like throwing water on a fire that is just about to spark. Not only that, your pores open up in the morning just as your body tries to grow energy. When you wash your hair at this time, you invite cold air and external elements to enter, well before you have had time to reach your energetic peak. There is a whole day of work to do, and instead of developing your energy, you consume the inventory of qi in the blood by taking a bath or shower. If your body's yang energy empties, you will become cold, and all kinds of illnesses will grow. Furthermore, the most important acupoints are concentrated in your head, where your brain is. If you must wash your hair early in the morning, at least wait to do it until after breakfast when you've had something to eat.

4. DO NOT EAT FRUIT INDISCRIMINATELY. Our spleen and stomach like to be warm, and that is when they can digest food and transport nutrients. Fruits are generally raw and cold, so they hurt the spleen and stomach when you eat them too early.

The time of the year is also important for eating fruit. Spring is not the season to eat lots of fruit. Nature wants the fruit to grow in the spring, mature in summer, and be harvested in fall, which is the best time to eat lots of fruit. Eating too much fruit in winter when the temperature is low and fruit is raw and cold can cause damage to the function of the spleen and stomach. That means you will not be able to digest and absorb as many nutrients as you normally would. Therefore, eat fruit in moderation.

Consider your body type as well. Fruits mature in different seasons (except for winter), but because of modern technology and global trade, we can eat fruit transported from different parts of the world to us. Thus, summer fruit from all over are available for us to eat in the winter. However, we must resist eating off-season. For example, eating watermelon in the winter is the opposite of what watermelon is supposed to do: relieve summer heat. Eating a "cold" type of fruit when your body is cold will hurt your kidneys and spleen, which will cause an energy deficiency.

For men, this is harmful in the long run. You might develop pain around your waist or back. Women may develop uterine-related problems, like period pain and the growth of polyps. If you belong to a cold body type, you should eat less fruit and avoid cold dishes. Cold dishes should only be eaten with wine.

Salad is considered raw and cold as well. Eating fruit and salad in order to lose weight and stay trim is not desirable for cold-body types: it will hurt your spleen and stomach and, ultimately, the normal absorption of nutrients.

We must follow our body type and seasons when we eat fruit: moderation is important, and following nature's path is essential.

5. **DO NOT GO TO THE GYM AFTER WORK.** TCM perceives this routine as damaging because at the end of the day, we have used up most of our yang energy. Between 7:00 p.m. and 9:00 p.m., our heart's qi is the most active as it tries to clean up the toxins and to rest up and prepare it for sleep. Therefore, exercise at that time is most inappropriate.

The best time to work out is the early morning when yang energy is strong and rising. If you have to exercise at night, take a walk. Exercising too vigorously at night is tantamount to damaging your health.

In terms of exercise intensity, opt for light and medium exercise between thirty and sixty minutes. Exercising until you sweat slightly will increase your blood circulation, whereas vigorous exercise makes you feel exhausted, which will hurt your qi.

Healthy exercise is moderate. People whose bodies are weaker (such as seniors and individuals who have gone through physical trauma) should do slow exercise like tai chi. This practice utilizing slow breath helps us to absorb and accumulate nature's energy. The movements move the muscles, and the breathing exercises move the organs.

A simple way to gain yang energy is to hold a big tree with your hands wrapped around it. Breathe deeply for as many minutes as you'd like. Old pine trees are especially wonderful for this purpose.

If you are wondering why we are not giving advice on how to increase your yin, that is because yin cannot be boosted through exercise or lifestyle changes. You must get yin from food or herbs. Men are rarely yin deficient.

The IMPACT of AIR-CONDITIONING

Humans are born with the ability to sustain the four seasons—cold or hot, wet or dry. But air-conditioning has changed the microclimate we live in.

Summers have become a battleground for our bodies as every public place we go to has its A/C set too high. When we are exposed to extreme heat outside and then step into an air-conditioned room, we become instantly cold. This is very unhealthy for us. Whereas the four seasons are gradual and slow, the artificial climate is sudden and abrupt, and our bodies have no time to adjust. What's worse, as we go in and out of A/C, we expose our body to continuous changes in temperature, too drastic for the human body to adjust to.

Have you noticed what happens to your skin during the summer? Imagine that you are outside under the blazing sun and you are sweating. Then you walk into the office or a store and the air suddenly becomes freezing cold. What happens to the sweat and perspiration that were assisting you in expelling the heat and toxins out of your body? They are now trapped under your skin. It is a common occurrence.

Your skin isn't the only organ affected by A/C. If you are wearing shorts or a skirt in an air-conditioned room, you are letting cold travel up your legs. Once it interacts with the trapped heat inside your body, your spleen and stomach will start having issues because the A/C passes cold dampness into our body.

Women need to be more cautious about what we wear in these situations. If our clothing is too thin or leaves our waist exposed, the cold from the exterior environment will penetrate through the meridians into our organs, especially the spleen and stomach. Women's bodies are so sensitive because our reproductive system is complicated. Menstruation requires our uterus to be kept warm to keep our hormonal cycle in equilibrium. If we are exposed to exterior cold, our circulation will be affected and our yang energy will stall. Our menstruation may not be as smooth, and blood that should be excreted may not exit our system properly. If it is repeatedly stuck within our bodies for too long, it can become detrimental for us over a long period of time.

I (Rose) was working as a chief financial officer for a six-hundred-plus employee organization, and the central air control for the whole floor was inside my private office. Every day, many colleagues knocked on my door asking me to adjust the temperature set by the A/C thermometer. It was high one moment and low the next. One person would complain that it was too cold, and the next would complain that it was too hot. The quarrels among my colleagues were unending. Finally at a staff meeting one day, I told them they were all too disruptive. They had been coming into my office nonstop, and the thermometer for the A/C system had gone crazy. My boss and I decided that the best thing to do was to take a poll to figure out the temperature most people preferred. Then we told them that that was it; we could not custom-fit the A/C to every individual's needs. I may have become the least popular person in the office that day.

We bring this story up to illustrate how differently people perceive temperature due to their body types and their yin and yang deficiencies.

The good news is that heating systems have no negative effects on the body because our organs are all warm!

DAMPNESS

In addition to yin and yang imbalances, dampness can be a cause of sickness according to TCM. It occurs when moisture is trapped inside the body. If your body fails to excrete it, the extra moisture will cause your organs to have issues. TCM believes that dampness is mucus trapped inside the organs that our bodies fail to get rid of.

Some common illnesses caused by dampness include diarrhea (dampness trapped inside the stomach) and rheumatoid arthritis (dampness trapped inside the joints). Everyday symptoms of dampness include fatigue, feeling bloated, having loose stool, and loss of appetite. You might ask, *How does this happen?*

In TCM, the theory is that the mucus we secrete contains toxins. If an individual is 100 percent healthy, the body will push out the toxins through sweat, urine, and bowel movements. If an organ is being affected by dampness, our body (especially our spleen) will fail to perform its functions correctly.

Vertigo, for example, is caused by dampness. According to Western medicine, this condition happens when there is excessive moisture buildup in the inner ears that causes the inner hair that is in charge of balance management to wilt. There are a few possible instigators of vertigo according to conventional Western medicine: calcium particles clumping up, Ménière's disease (an inner ear disorder), or an infection. TCM believes the cause of vertigo is dampness trapped inside the ear.

One of the most popular treatments Western doctors prescribe for vertigo symptoms is motion sickness drugs. TCM, however, treats vertigo with herbs that take away the moisture in the ear by forcing the body to gradually excrete the moisture via urine and bodily waste. The TCM method is more permanent: it is believed that once the moisture is gone, the hair within the inner ear can stand up again and not wilt.

TCM theorizes that cancer occurs when serious mucus congestion takes place inside an organ. After a while, the toxin in the mucus causes changes in the cells of the organ and ultimately becomes cancer. Since cancer is viewed as a heat-related body issue, a series of cold herbs is prescribed to clear out the toxins. Practitioners often advise the patient to stay away from cold food and to try to gain yang qi, which he or she is likely deficient in. More qi can help energize the organs to move out the toxins. In situations like this, it's best to eat cold and neutral foods. Milk should be avoided, because it causes mucus buildup and is considered an extremely damp food.

In daily life, we should be conscious of damp foods and eat them in moderation. And we should try to drink soups that clear the dampness, a good self-care routine to keep ourselves healthy.

CAUSES OF DAMPNESS

Two things can cause dampness in your body: something you ate or drank or the environment around you.

Perhaps you recently consumed milk, clams, crabs, shellfish, dairy products, oranges, or plums. These are all foods that foster dampness.

As we've already learned, your exterior environment can be natural or artificial. Hong Kong, where our families are from, is damp because of the high humidity. Thus, people who live there suffer from illnesses caused by dampness more frequently than, say, someone who lives in a desert climate like Arizona.

Artificially, we create dampness in our environment through air-conditioning. Having it on 24/7 is extremely injurious to health. When you hear about people who suffer from neck pain and pain in the muscles for no apparent reason, the cause is often dampness and cold trapped inside their bodies.

Sometimes this is not our fault. Dampness can be caused by our occupations. Fishermen and divers, for example, are exposed to dampness and cold all the time. As they age, they will feel pain in their joints or legs or have headaches more frequently than the average person. A caregiver friend of ours came down with arthritis in her legs when she was sixty-five; it turns out she had spent her youth farming in rice paddy fields.

Overexposing yourself to ocean and water exercises will also result in the same problems. People with dampness should avoid living next to oceans and lakes, which are considered high-humidity exterior environments. Headaches can result if dampness enters the head and gets trapped.

DAMPNESS AND THE SEASONS

The dampness you feel differs by season. In the northern hemisphere, the heaviest dampness occurs in the spring, when the dampness is slightly cold. There is humidity from the rain, and the air is usually heavier. We call this "cold dampness." Cold dampness affects you differently from "heat dampness" (caused by hot temperatures), although the symptoms and side effects may be similar. Spring dampness causes you to feel tired because your yang energy is suppressed by the dampness and cannot circulate. Thus, fatigue is common in the spring, and you want to sleep more.

Summer's heat dampness is caused by hot temperatures and when humidity increases with heat. Shortness of breath, heart discomfort, and a suffocated feeling are all symptoms of this variety of dampness. Avoid eating cold and raw food during this time. Eating ginger (in the morning only) will help expel dampness too, but ginger may not suit everybody (see pages 177–81 for more details). Carrots and water chestnuts are also good for driving heat and dampness away during summertime.

Fall has very little dampness because it is a dry season and usually does not accommodate dampness.

Dampness returns in the winter, caused by the cold mixed with snow and rain, and this calls for different treatment. Other than drinking the soups we recommend in the upcoming chapters, you can do other things to keep your body warm and healthy:

- Drink some ginger tea with rock sugar and red dates.
- Exercise regularly to drive up the immune system to expel the cold and dampness.
- Sit under the sun daily to increase your yang energy.
- Before going to sleep, soak your legs in a container filled with hot water for fifteen minutes. This will also help you to banish any dampness, keep your body warm, improve your circulation, and relax your mind so you will have a peaceful sleep.

These foods and herbs drive away dampness year-round:

- Adzuki beans
- Apples
- Carrots
- Coix seeds
- Hyacinth beans
- Makhana
- Wild yam

Avoid "cold" food, sweet food, fatty food, and fried food during the damp seasons. Anything served cold is not desirable either.

FIRE

Fire is the third main cause of illness in Traditional Chinese Medicine. "Fire," used here, describes heat trapped in the body that causes one to feel "on fire."

Perhaps you've experienced the symptoms firsthand. You feel dry, or your temperament has taken a turn for the worse without any explanation. You may suddenly have bouts of anxiety and frustration. Other symptoms might include gum swelling, canker sores, pimples, very yellow urine, red eyes, and a slightly sore throat. If you are dealing with any of these issues, chances are the heat in your body is off balance: your yin and yang are out of equilibrium.

According to TCM, some common culprits of having too much fire in the body include:

- Too much fatty and deep-fried food, such as potato chips, fried chicken, and barbecue
- Too much hot and spicy food with chiles
- Sleeping late, which can cause you to build up heat
- Stress and anxiety

❀   **Healing Herbal Soups**

The probability of a heat imbalance is heightened during the summer and can be exacerbated by poor eating habits. Not only do you feel hot internally during this time, but the external environment is also hot. These two factors can cause you to feel heated up inside.

FOODS TO FAN OUT THE FLAMES

When all these symptoms show up and make you feel uncomfortable, you need relief. The solution is to eat a lot of special food and soup to reduce your heat. Eating too much "hot" food without balancing or neutralizing it with "cool" or "cold" food will kick your "heat" levels into high gear. Obviously you want to avoid this.

Here are some of the more effective foods that help to bring down the heat in your body:

1. **BITTER MELON.** Bitter melon contains unique bitter gourd glycosides, which can dispel heat and strengthen the heart. It's a great remedy for stomach flus, damp-heat dysentery, vomiting, diarrhea, and hematuria. The bitter melon detoxifies the liver and gallbladder, brings down gastrointestinal fire, and cleanses your body in general. If you have symptoms, such as sore throat, bad breath, or red eyes, some bitter melon might be good for you.

2. **CELERY.** Celery can clear away heat and detoxify. It contains a lot of crude fiber, which can stimulate gastrointestinal motility and is also good for laxative detoxification. Since it is a cold type of food, individuals with cold body types should eat it in moderation. Individuals with low blood pressure and cold body types should be more cautious about consuming celery because it is powerful when it comes to lowering blood pressure.

3. **CUCUMBERS.** The average cucumber has the highest water content of all vegetables: 96 to 98 percent. The cellulose contained in cucumbers is very soft and promotes the excretion of spoiled food in the intestines and the lowering of cholesterol. In addition, cucumbers clear heat and conserve water, so they are excellent for the summer.

4. **HONEY.** Nutrient-rich honey is considered a neutral type of food. Honey itself moisturizes the intestines, coupled with the ability to clear heat and detoxify. It calms your nerves. In addition, it is a magical sweetener that restores beauty and is especially beneficial for women. In the summer, Chinese people combine honey with honeysuckle and chrysanthemum flowers as a drink to clear away the heat, drop the "fire," and detox.

5. **HONEYSUCKLE FLOWERS.** Dried honeysuckle flowers, a popular herbal beverage for Chinese families during the height of summer, are often mixed with chrysanthemum flowers to make a drink to clear the heat. The combination reduces fire and relaxes the whole body. In Chinese, honeysuckle is nicknamed "the little fairy in the medicine shop." It is perfect

for dampness and heat stagnation, dry mouth and throat, constipation, and red eyes. Also, if your urine feels hot and your stool seems more odoriferous than usual, drinking a cup of honeysuckle a day will help to quickly clear these symptoms.

6. **LOTUS SEEDS.** Lotus seeds are known to lower the fire and calm people. They clear out the heart's toxins and are great for nourishing the mind. They can also strengthen the intestines and stomach. During summer, when the heart is at its strongest, the heat can make you feel irritable and anxious. Adding lotus seeds to soups, drinks, or desserts can help you feel better. In Chinese cuisine, lotus seeds are often eaten together with lily bulbs in soups, desserts, and drinks. Try to buy the variety with the skin on, as opposed to the skinless ones. Lily bulbs can complement lotus seeds very well because both have the same calming effect on the nerves and work together to clear out toxins.

7. **PEARS.** Both regular pears and Chinese pears (also known as snow pears) are extremely effective. Try pear juice or pear puree, or add pears to soups.

8. **TEA.** Several types of flower teas can relieve the summer heat. (See Chapter 10 for more on tea.)

9. **TURNIPS.** Drinking turnip soup is another way to drop the fire. But be aware that turnip is a very cold food, so people with cold bodies need to eat this vegetable in moderation.

10. **WATERMELON.** Watermelon is sweet and considered a cold food. Especially during the summer, it should be your first choice for clearing heat and quenching thirst. When you have heatstroke, fever, or feel dehydrated, watermelon can rejuvenate you. Eating a moderate amount of watermelon nourishes your yin and clears fire, but eating too much of it can cause diuresis and a yin deficiency. People with cold body types need to be cautious when consuming watermelon and should eat only a moderate amount. People with weak and sensitive spleens and stomachs should also not eat too much watermelon, which can easily lead to diarrhea and bloating.

The following foods help with heat but are not quite as effective as the ones just listed:

- Aloe vera
- Duck
- Eggplant
- Mung beans
- Soybeans
- Tomato

3

SLEEPING *and* RESTING

HOW *to* SLEEP CORRECTLY

A widely held belief is that we need six to eight hours of sleep every night. But did you know that the time at which you go to bed determines your overall health? According to Traditional Chinese Medicine, our organs take turns to rest and perform their functions. This means that if you want optimal health, you must sleep during certain hours and be awake during others.

Here is a breakdown of those hours:

11:00 P.M.-1:00 A.M.: The gallbladder resets. This is most effective when the body is at rest.

1:00 A.M.-3:00 A.M.: The liver detoxes. Make sure you are asleep so the body can focus on that. Staying up this late is extremely harmful. If you neglect to sleep during these hours, you will become unsettled and angry over time. When the liver is not healthy, your eyes will also suffer.

3:00 A.M-5:00 A.M.: The lungs rejuvenate. While this is happening, the lungs store yin energy, so people with lung issues may experience coughing during these hours even if they are asleep. It is important to keep warm because breathing in cold air hurts the lungs.

5:00 A.M.-7:00 A.M.: The large intestines do the bulk of their work at this time. Strong bowels in the morning are a sign that you are in good health because your body is ready to expel all the toxins it has accrued from the day before.

7:00 A.M.-9:00 A.M.: The stomach is at its height of functionality, so this is the best time to eat. Breakfast should be nutritious and hot because warming up your stomach is of utmost importance. Congee and oatmeal are excellent choices. We should try to eat slowly to encourage better absorption. Because the sun is rising, the yang qi is good. You should exercise and breathe in the fresh morning air in order to absorb nature's energy.

9:00 A.M.-11:00 A.M.: It's the spleen's turn to work. Enzymes are released to help digest food, and energy is circulated throughout the rest of the body for the day ahead. This is the time to complete tasks at the office. Stay away from chiles and other oily and spicy foods.

11:00 A.M.-1:00 P.M.: Our heart realigns. Take a break, eat a light lunch, and let the qi in your heart grow. When the heart is energetic, you will feel refreshed and ready to work in the afternoon.

1:00 P.M.-3:00 P.M.: After lunch, the small intestine revs up. By now, your lunch will be digested. Water is transported to the bladder while the intestines move the waste slowly into the large intestines. The nutrients generated from the food go to the spleen, which will disseminate energy throughout the body.

3:00 P.M.–5:00 P.M.: The bladder starts working and will move all the unwanted materials out of the body. It is the perfect time to drink some water to replenish your system.

5:00 P.M.–7:00 P.M.: The kidneys pick up. We should relax and wind down. A good use of this time is to prepare dinner and spend time with your family and friends.

7:00 P.M.–9:00 P.M.: The meridian around the heart area begins the bulk of its work. Think serene thoughts to keep your vibration high and maybe take a stroll to bask in nature. Do not do strenuous exercise, and avoid sweating too much.

9:00 P.M.–11:00 P.M.: The lymphatic system and immune system check up on each other. Refrain from snacking. It is unhealthy to force your gallbladder to work while it is ready for rest. It is bad for your sleep too, since your body is being coerced into digesting the food.

Now that you are aware of the body's timetable, try to coordinate your activities in a way to complement the natural cycle of life. Working against it will result in the deterioration of your health and organs. Be cognizant, and your body will resist aging faster than is necessary.

If you make a sincere effort to work together with your body, you will see and experience a more vivacious, healthy, and younger you in no time.

GOOD SLEEP *vs.* BAD SLEEP

The Chinese saying, "A person who sleeps three times a day will shorten their life span," means that not all sleep is good for you. Obviously this is an exaggeration. But there are two kinds of sleep you need to be aware of: good sleep and bad sleep.

SLEEPING IN

Some people love to sleep until noon. This is not healthy because morning is the time when the yang energy rises and grows. We should wake up to absorb this energy by working out.

When we sleep late, we often miss breakfast, the most important meal of the day. If you skip breakfast, you will cause problems for your intestines and will set back your energy levels for the rest of the day. This is akin to driving to work on an empty gas tank. If the car doesn't have fuel, how is it going to drive well?

Food gives us energy, and this energy, together with the sun's energy in the morning, combines to become the yang qi in our body.

SLEEPING WHEN YOU ARE ANGRY OR UNHAPPY

It's understandable: you had an argument with your spouse or are experiencing sad feelings from your job, so you take a nap to "forget" about what happened during the day. This is harmful because you bring this negative energy into your sleep . The negative energy will cause you to secrete toxins in your body, and the toxins will harm your organs since resting time is when your organs realign.

SLEEPING AFTER A MEAL

Most people feel sleepy after a meal. We often see this around the holidays when there are big feasts. But after a meal, your food needs to be digested. If you go to sleep at this time, there will be a lack of oxygen for your head as it draws all the blood to the digestive system instead. If you have to sleep, wait thirty minutes after a meal. And for seniors only, taking a short nap after lunch is good for the body.

Knowing these rules does not mean that if you are not sleeping at a certain time, it will be horrible for you. All of us have own own natural clock, so sleeping patterns vary with the individual. Overall, a well-disciplined and organized lifestyle is always a path to good health. That is why humans have three meals, wake up in the morning, and sleep at night. It's what nature intended.

HOW *to* BOIL SOUP *and* WHERE *to* BUY INGREDIENTS

ow that you understand the basic concepts behind Traditional Chinese Medicine, body types, and food energies, it's time to boil your first herbal soup!

BOILING 101

We'll start with the cookware. The key to boiling is to find a pot that does not cause too many chemical reactions. For that reason, use a clay earthenware pot. If you don't have one, you can use an enamelware or a stainless-steel pot. We're also big fans of crockpots, but make sure you don't use the enameled cast-iron kind because iron and copper pots encourage the wrong types of chemical reactions (toxic ones), especially when Chinese herbs are involved.

Clay pots are our preference because they have stable chemical properties, uniform heating, slow heat transfer, and less evaporation during cooking. The pots seldom overheat and burn out its contents. Porcelain pots are good too.

Because cracks form when clay pots experience sudden temperature fluctuations, a clay pot that has just been used for cooking should not be washed immediately with cold water. Allow the pot to cool down for several minutes before cleaning. When washing the pot, note that any oil stains on it cannot be soaked off with detergent. Instead, wipe the pot with leftover tea leaves. Alternatively, you can soak the pot in rice water and then heat it up. After it cools down, scrub the pot with a brush.

Should you decide to use our second choice, a stainless-steel pot, keep in mind that steel transfers heat very fast, so make sure you use low heat to simmer your ingredients. Otherwise the ingredients will not be cooked long enough and the nutrients will not be released properly. Another word of caution is that stainless-steel pots dry up soup fast if you do not watch the fire closely.

In traditional Chinese cooking, we measure soup and water with "bowls." A bowl of water is equal to one cup of water. A standard serving of soup is thought of as one bowl, or one cup, of soup.

Always use room-temperature water when boiling Chinese herbal soups. And when the soup is boiling, pay close attention to the heat levels. In general, you must use high heat to boil. As it reaches a simmer, turn the heat to low because only slow cooking can bring out the taste and the contents of the ingredients effectively.

Boil soup with the lid on. Obviously if the liquid boils over, remove the lid until it simmers down. Then turn the heat down to low and replace the lid. Do not cheat yourself by boiling soup without the lid on!

Finally, we often instruct cooks to boil the soup and reduce the broth to the number of bowls specified in the recipe. If the soup boils down to the desired cups faster than we estimate in the recipe, just remove the pot from the heat earlier.

If you are short on time, we recommend that you buy an automatic Chinese soup cooker. These are excellent because they ensure perfect boiling. All you have to do is put all the ingredients in the cooker, turn on the timer, and the soup will be ready for you when you want it. The appliances are available at Chinese herbal stores or supermarkets. If you do use an automatic cooker, use 25 percent less water than the recipe recommends because soup cookers tend to evaporate less water and conserve more liquid. However, use the same cooking time that we suggest in the recipe.

Do not use the automatic soup cooker for recipes that contain fish. For recipes that contain snow fungus or fish maw, you can still use the automatic soup cooker but you must prepare these ingredients ahead of time.

When it comes time to clean the herbs, just rinse them with water. Do not use soap!

Finally, drink the soup hot. It's good to keep your stomach warm at all times. If you must reheat the soup, use a saucepan rather than the microwave. Most often, you can eat some of the ingredients in the soup if you want (and we identify which ones for each recipe), but the broth is the most important part.

WHERE *to* PURCHASE HERBS *and* COOKWARE

We usually buy our herbs in person from Chinese herbal pharmacies in Los Angeles. These types of shops are usually located in Chinatowns and Chinese communities in major cities. And since we are so familiar with herbs, it is not a problem for us to find the ingredients we are looking for.

We recommend that you buy the herbs the same way. If this is your first time going to an establishment like this, take our book with you. Identify the Chinese name of the herb that is listed in the mini-encyclopedia of our book (see Chapter 5). Then tell the store clerk what you want to buy by showing him or her the name of the herb in Chinese in case this person does not speak English.

Your first visit may be confusing, and that is part of the learning experience. To illustrate what you might encounter, here is an example of a shopping trip you may take. Say you want to buy coix seeds (pearl barley). When you get to the store, you locate the seeds but notice there are two types. However, the packages before you do not say what type of coix seeds they are, cooked or raw, so you ask the store clerk for help. The clerk may stare at you with a blank expression. Perhaps he doesn't know what you're talking about. Show him the Chinese characters that correspond to the type of coix seeds you want to buy (cooked coix seeds). If you're wondering about the differences between the seeds, raw coix seeds are slightly cold and not suitable for cold body types, so we mostly recommend cooked coix seeds. No matter what you end up with, it is not going to harm you, but the effect is not as good as if you had used the cooked kind.

If you feel a trip to the store is too daunting or you live very far from one, your other choice is to buy the products through an herbal emporium online. Be careful to make sure the website you are using is dependable and sells good-quality products. Herbs can vary a lot in terms of quality, and it's possible that the descriptions for products are intended for a Chinese audience and may be vague for non-Chinese speakers.

In light of these considerations, we have set up a website (www.healingherbal soups.com) to help you obtain most of the ingredients for our soup recipes. We have worked out an arrangement with a dependable Chinese herb supplier to make sure all the herbs for a particular recipe will be packaged together. That way you can order the herb package based on the soup name, which will save you a tremendous amount of hassle. The website also includes cookware for purchase. We believe we have chosen ones that are both reliable and economical for you.

We promise you that boiling Chinese herbal soups will be an unusual experience to expand your palate and open your eyes to the world of culinary healing.

Drink up!

CHAPTER

5

FIELD GUIDE
to INGREDIENTS

30

28

37

35

32

34

20

36

31

38

39

33

41b

41a

42

40

21

45

43

44

The soup recipes in this book use various Chinese herbs, vegetables, fruits, meats, and poultry, and unless you are Chinese, you may never have heard of some of them.

A list of select ingredients with their Chinese and English names follows, and it will come in handy when you go shopping for items at Chinese groceries and apothecaries. Western supermarkets may carry something similar, but it is hard to tell if you have the right product, so we advise you to stick to Chinese establishments.

If you wish to speak to a store clerk and are unsure of whether to refer to an herb by its Chinese or English name, always go with the Chinese nomenclature.

KEY	CHINESE NAME	FOOD TYPE	ENGLISH NAME	PRODUCT FORM
1	赤小豆	Neutral	Adzuki beans	Dried
2	北杏	Slightly warm	(Bitter) Apricot kernels	Dried
3	南杏	Neutral	(Sweet) Apricot kernels	Dried
4	黃芪	Slightly warm	Astragalus root	Dried
5	黑豆	Neutral	Black beans	Dried (not canned)
6	眉豆	Neutral	Black-eyed peas	Dried
7	合掌瓜/佛手瓜	Cool	Chayote	Fresh
8	山楂	Slightly warm	Chinese hawthorn	Dried
9	甘草	Neutral	Chinese licorice	Dried
10	山藥/淮山	Neutral	Chinese yam (common yam rhizome)	Fresh (a) or dried (b)
11	黨參	Neutral	Codonopsis root	Dried
12	薏米	Slightly cool	Coix seeds	Raw or roasted
13	灯芯花	Cold	Common rush	Dried
14	響螺	Cool	Conch meat	Dried
15	螺頭	Cool	Conch head	Dried
16	虫草花	Neutral	Cordyceps flowers	Dried
17	麥冬	Cold	Dwarf lilyturf	Dried
18	五指毛桃	Slightly warm	Five-finger peach	Dried
19	川貝	Slightly cold	Fritillaria bulbs	Dried
20	節瓜	Neutral	Fuzzy melon	Fresh

Healing Herbal Soups

21	薑	Warm	Ginger	Fresh
22	银杏	Neutral	Ginkgo nuts	Frozen or dried
23	枸杞	Neutral	Goji berries	Dried
24	金银花	Cold	Honeysuckle	Dried
25	扁豆	Neutral	Hyacinth beans	Dried
26	扁豆花	Neutral	Hyacinth bean flowers	Dried
27	木綿花	Cool	Kapok flowers	Dried
28	藿香	Slightly warm	Korean mint	Dried
29	百合	Slightly cold	Lily bulbs	Fresh (a) or dried (b)
30	桂圓肉	Warm	Longan pulp	Dried
31	茨實	Neutral	Makhana	Dried
32	羅漢果	Cool	Monk fruit	Dried
33	鷓鴣	Slightly warm	Partridge	Fresh poultry
34	玉竹	Neutral	Polygonatum	Dried
35	茯苓	Neutral	Poria mushroom	Dried
36	紅棗	Warm	Red dates (jujube)	Dried
37	赤靈芝	Slightly warm	Red lingzhi (Reishi mushroom)	Dried
38	茅根	Cold	Rhizoma imperatae	Dried
39	沙參	Slightly cold	Sand ginseng	Dried
40	海底椰	Cold	Sea coconut (double coconut)	Dried
41	雪梨	Cold	Snow pear	Fresh (a) or dried (b)
42	竹蔗	Cold	Sugarcane	Fresh or dried
43	陳皮	Warm	Tangerine peel	Dried (do not use fresh)
44	土茯苓	Neutral	Tuckahoe	Fresh or Dried
45	雪耳	Neutral	White snow fungus	Dried

INGREDIENT DESCRIPTIONS

赤小豆
ADZUKI BEANS

Adzuki beans are deep red and purple. They have a mild, nutty taste with a sweet quality that makes them a popular ingredient for Asian desserts. The beans are soft but not completely smooth in texture and have a mealy feel.

Adzuki beans can invigorate the spleen and remove dampness, disperse blood, and detoxify. They contain a variety of nutrients, including protein, carbohydrates, calcium, and phosphorus. Adzuki beans come from a vine that grows during the warm season and have been cultivated for centuries in China and Japan.

WHERE TO BUY: Chinese supermarkets.

北杏
(BITTER) APRICOT KERNELS

Because bitter apricot kernels contain more cyanide than sweet ones, we usually add only a spoonful or two of it to our soups. The anti-asthmatic effect of bitter apricot kernels is stronger than that of sweet apricot kernels. Bitter apricot kernels are suitable for coughs, asthma, intestinal dryness, and constipation. A bitter apricot kernel is thinner and smaller than that of a sweet apricot kernel. Its shape is flat, and it is left-right asymmetric. Apricots are mostly grown in northeast and northwest China and some in Mongolia, in hilly areas or low mountains where the climate is cold.

WHERE TO BUY: Chinese supermarkets, herbal pharmacies.

南杏
(SWEET) APRICOT KERNELS

The apricot kernel is the seed inside the apricot pit. Although it is widely used in Chinese cuisine and medicine, recent studies have found that the seeds contain amygdalin, a poisonous compound. Amygdalin can be broken down into cyanide, which is toxic. However, the cyanide in the apricot kernel is bound up in such a way that it is sequestered inside the seed and is released only when it is crushed.

There are two types of apricot kernels: sweet and bitter. Sweet apricot seeds contain very little or no amygdalin. Further processing of the seed like grinding, soaking, then heating the seeds can neutralize the toxin. Sweet kernels moisturize the lungs and relieve coughs and asthma. They can also produce body fluid and boost appetite and are especially suitable for seniors. The seeds are grown in Southern China.

WHERE TO BUY: Chinese supermarkets, herbal pharmacies.

黄芪

ASTRAGALUS ROOT

Found growing in parts of the northeast and northwest of China, astragalus root has been a foundational herb in TCM for hundreds of years. The antioxidant replenishes qi and strengthens the heart and capillaries, lowers blood pressure, is antibacterial, and improves muscle strength.

Pregnant woman, who are hot body types, cannot take this herb because it encourages the fetus to grow too much, causing difficulty with delivery. People with the flu or a cold should also avoid it until they are well.

WHERE TO BUY: Chinese herbal pharmacies.

黑豆

BLACK BEANS

Chinese black beans are fermented black soybeans. They are not the same as Mexican black beans, which are black turtle beans. Chinese ones are dried and come in a package, not in a can.

Chinese black beans tonify the kidneys and spleen and nourish the internal organs. They can prevent constipation, improve immunity, clean blood vessels, and possess antioxidant and anti-aging properties. The beans have a high protein content and contain soy isoflavones, which stimulate female hormones. The legumes are also rich in vitamin B complex and vitamin E, which is believed to contribute to beauty and youthfulness. Since they contain a great deal of pantothenic acid, Chinese black beans are helpful for dark-haired people who do not want their hair to turn white.

People with serious kidney problems should avoid them because they are not easy to digest, and those with gout should not have them either. It is not advisable to eat beans together with soy milk, spinach, and milk. For soup-making, do not buy the black beans that are salted.

WHERE TO BUY: Chinese supermarkets.

眉豆

BLACK-EYED PEAS

Black-eyed peas contain a great deal of carbohydrates that can be converted into energy, regulate metabolism, and help in excreting toxins in the body. In TCM, they are believed to help cure diarrhea, reduce swelling, and expel dampness. Black-eyed peas also warm the stomach and spleen. They grow in many parts of China and are popular in the southern United States.

WHERE TO BUY: Chinese supermarkets, herbal pharmacies.

合掌瓜
CHAYOTE

Chayote are rich in amino acids and vitamin C. The squash is believed to increase immunity against illness, lower blood pressure, and improve intelligence in children because it is rich in zinc. A relative of the cucumber family, the fruit has a bland taste but is often stir-fried in Chinese dishes. Chayote can be found growing in Central and South America, Asia, and Australia.

WHERE TO BUY: Chinese supermarkets.

山楂
CHINESE HAWTHORN

The berries from Chinese hawthorn, which taste a bit like crabapples, can significantly reduce serum cholesterol and triglycerides and effectively prevent atherosclerosis. The total flavonoids in the herb can also expand coronary blood vessels, increase coronary blood flow, reduce myocardial oxygen consumption, and permanently lower blood pressure. The plant is mostly found in northern China and is known for being a major ingredient of traditional Chinese candies called haw flakes. Chinese hawthorn berries are not suitable for people with hyperacidity in their stomach.

WHERE TO BUY: Chinese herbal pharmacies.

甘草
CHINESE LICORICE

The root of Chinese licorice is considered one of the fifty fundamental TCM herbs. It can detoxify over twelve hundred kinds of toxins, remove phlegm, and has pain relief and anticancer effects. Chinese licorice should not be confused with licorice from Europe and America. The scientific name for Chinese licorice is *Glycyrrhiza uralensis*.

Licorice also nourishes the spleen, strengthens qi, relieves coughs, moisturizes the lungs, and harmonizes other herbs. It can be found growing on dry grasslands and sunny hillsides. The herb is grown in places like Shaanxi, Gansu, Qinghai, Xinjiang, and Shandong, China.

WHERE TO BUY: Chinese herbal pharmacies.

山藥 / 淮山
CHINESE YAM (COMMON YAM RHIZOME)

Chinese yam is plucked in the winter after the stalk and leaves have withered. It nourishes the spleen and stomach and restores the functions of the lungs and kidneys. Not just for medicinal purposes, stir-fried Chinese yam is a popular dish throughout China. The perennial climbing vine is farmed in China, Korea, and Japan.

WHERE TO BUY: Chinese supermarkets for fresh yam. We recommend buying yams grown in China only. Dried yam can be found in grocery stores and herbal pharmacies.

黨參
CODONOPSIS ROOT

Codonopsis root is one of the most famous and widely used herbs in TCM. It restores qi and invigorates the spleen and lungs, and it can remediate shortness of breath, heart palpitations, and coughing due to a deficiency of qi. Codonopsis is grown in northwestern Sichuan, Qinghai, Gansu, and Shaanxi in China. The plant is usually found in mountain forests, at forest edges, and in bushes between 1500 and 3200 meters above sea level.

WHERE TO BUY: Chinese herbal pharmacies.

薏米
COIX SEEDS

Coix seeds, which come in raw and roasted varieties, clear dampness and strengthen the spleen. The herb has high nutritional and medicinal value. In addition to being rich in high-quality protein, carbohydrates, fats, mineral elements, and vitamins, coix seeds are rich in polysaccharides. They are found to lower blood sugar and scavenge free radicals.

Coix grows near wetlands and streams in hot and humid weather. They are sourced from different parts of China, India, and Southeast Asia.

WHERE TO BUY: Chinese supermarkets, herbal pharmacies.

灯芯花
COMMON RUSH

Common rush can reduce heart fire, stop bleeding, and reduce swelling. It is often prepared with other herbs to remove dampness. The flower grows near swamps and can be located in many parts of China. It is slightly cold in nature so people with cold bodies should avoid taking it.

WHERE TO FIND: Chinese herbal pharmacies.

響螺
CONCH

Conch is a large, edible sea snail. The meat from the mollusk can invigorate the spleen and stomach and nourish your skin, blood, liver, and kidneys. It is rich in protein and inorganic salts, as well as a variety of vitamins. Conch contains an important substance for maintaining and improving the body's immunity and is used to relieve backaches and heal impotence and spermatorrhea caused by kidney qi deficiencies.

Dried conch is preferred over fresh for boiling soup. It should not be taken with Western medicines like oxytetracycline. It should not be eaten with beef, mutton, clams, winter melon, cantaloupe, or fungus or drunk with ice water, as it will cause diarrhea.

WHERE TO BUY: Chinese herbal pharmacies.

虫草花
CORDYCEPS FLOWERS

Cordyceps are considered a fungus. They can enhance the immunity of the upper respiratory tract, relieve coughs, and prevent bronchitis. Since cordyceps belong to the mushroom family, they are high in fiber. They can lower cholesterol, clear stool, and help in intestinal peristalsis. They are grown in Asia.

WHERE TO BUY: Chinese herbal pharmacies.

麥冬
DWARF LILYTURF

The roots of the dwarf lilyturf plant are wonderful for restoring stomach fluids, supporting the spleen's qi, and transferring energy to the lungs. It also increases yin energy in the body. In TCM, the herb is used to restore the pancreatic production of insulin. However, it is quite powerful so practitioners advise people to take it once in a blue moon only.

The plant can be found growing in damp areas by hillside grass and beside streams in China, India, Japan, and Vietnam.

WHERE TO BUY: Chinese herbal pharmacies.

五指毛桃
FIVE-FINGER PEACH

Unlike the name that this plant has been given, five-finger peach has nothing to do with the fruit it is named after. In its natural state, the shrub's leaves look like five fingers, its leaves have fine hairs, and the tree bears fruit that looks like peaches when they are ripe.

Five-finger peach is known to invigorate the spleen, restore lung function, remove dampness, replenish qi, and strengthen the body overall. It can be used to treat symptoms such as loss of appetite, indigestion, coughs, and even to suppress tumor growth. The plant is widely planted in China and Bhutan. The herb's natural habitat is in canyons, next to streams, and in forests.

WHERE TO BUY: Chinese herbal pharmacies.

川貝
FRITILLARIA BULBS

Fritillaria bulbs have bitter, sweet, and slightly cold properties, according to TCM. The bulb is white in color and is known to cure coughs because it can clear heat, moisturize the lungs, and dispel phlegm. It is found in China, and in the Himalayas of India, Nepal, and Pakistan, as well as Japan, Korea, and Southeast Asia.

WHERE TO BUY: Chinese herbal pharmacies.

節瓜
FUZZY MELON

Fuzzy melon is a vegetable and a staple of Chinese cuisine. Available year-round, it is grown in many parts of China, Asia, and Mexico. It is produced on vines in warm climates.

Fuzzy melon is sweet in taste and neutral in nature. It helps in the production of body fluids, quenches thirst, relieves heat and dampness, invigorates the spleen and stomach, and improves bowel movements.

WHERE TO BUY: Chinese supermarkets.

银杏果
GINKGO NUTS

Perhaps you've heard about gingko biloba supplements that are made from this plant's leaves. What about ginkgo nuts? They are also a product of the ginkgo tree. A neutral food, ginkgo nuts are both sweet and bitter in taste. The nuts conserve qi in the lungs, calm coughs, and reduce frequent urination. They can treat asthma, phlegm coughs, gonorrhea, and other diseases. The nuts contain antioxidants that fight inflammation. The flavanol content in gingko nuts is believed to improve circulation, heart health, and blood flow to the brain, thus supporting brain function and improving dementia.

Gingko trees can be found growing in temperate and subtropical regions of China, Korea, Japan, North America, and Australia. Raw ginkgo seeds are toxic, so they should not be used in large doses or for long periods of time. Because of this, children and pregnant women are advised not to consume it.

WHERE TO BUY: Chinese herbal pharmacies.

枸杞
GOJI BERRIES

Goji berries are excellent immune system boosters and possess anticancer capabilities. This superfood can prevent and suppress tumors and prevent atherosclerosis. It's a great source of beta-carotene and a precursor to vitamin A formation. Legend is that hundreds of years ago, Buddhist monks in Tibet discovered the berries and ate them for longevity.

The fruit is found along the Silk Route regions in China like Ningxia, Xinjiang, Qinghai, Gansu, Inner Mongolia, Heilongjiang, and Jilin.

WHERE TO BUY: Chinese supermarkets, herbal pharmacies.

金银花
HONEYSUCKLE

Honeysuckle, a cold energy food, is sweet in taste. It can enhance immunity, lower blood lipids, and clear heat in the body. The plant also possesses anti-inflammatory and antibacterial functions. Drinks made with the flowers are best to consume during the summer. Since honeysuckle is a cold food, cold body types should limit their intake of it, especially women during menstruation. The flowers are found in southern China, Hainan Island, and parts of Burma and India.

WHERE TO BUY: Chinese herbal pharmacies.

扁豆
HYACINTH BEANS

Hyacinth beans are not technically a bean but the seed of the hyacinth plant, which is a rope-like vine. The seeds clear summer heat, remove dampness, and strengthen the spleen and the stomach. Originating from India, hyacinth beans can be found growing in Southeast Asia, China, and Africa.

WHERE TO BUY: Chinese herbal pharmacies.

扁豆花
HYACINTH BEAN FLOWERS

The flowers of the hyacinth bean perform similar functions as the hyacinth bean. They help with relieving summer heat, clearing dampness, and tempering the spleen and stomach.

WHERE TO BUY: Chinese herbal pharmacies.

❀   **Healing Herbal Soups**

木綿花
KAPOK FLOWERS

Kapok is the city flower of Guangzhou, China. When kapoks bloom in the spring, the streets are filled with red flowers that are a beautiful sight. There is even a festival that honors them in southern China. Kapok flowers are especially good in clearing spring and summer heat and dampness in humid weather. They can also detoxify.

WHERE TO BUY: Chinese herbal pharmacies.

藿香
KOREAN MINT

Korean mint is known to remove dampness from the body, especially summer dampness. The herb is a slightly warm food that can stop vomiting and clear heat. Korean mint also provides relief from fever and fatigue resulting from summer heat. If you put one leaf of the mint in your mouth, it can eliminate bad breath, prevent infectious diseases, and can be used as a preservative. People who are alcohol intolerant and children under age two should take the herb with caution.

WHERE TO BUY: Chinese herbal pharmacies.

百合
LILY BULBS

Lily bulbs originated in China but are now grown in North America and Europe. They are known to nourish yin qi and restore lung functions, as well as calm the heart and the mind. The plant has an excellent reputation for breaking prolonged coughs, reducing heart palpitations, and healing insomnia and damp energy sores.

WHERE TO BUY: Chinese herbal pharmacies for dry lily bulbs; frozen section of Chinese supermarkets for fresh lily bulbs.

桂圓肉
LONGAN PULP

Longan is a fruit and can be eaten raw. The meat is sweet in taste and is a warm energy food. It can improve appetite, nourish the blood and spleen, replenish the heart and calm nerves, and improve brainpower. Don't eat dried longan pulp when you are experiencing indigestion or if you feel you have phlegm in your stomach or spleen.

Longan grows in southern and western China, Southeast Asia, and warm and humid regions. The fruit is a bit like a grape in taste and texture but much muskier.

WHERE TO BUY: Chinese supermarkets (fresh), herbal pharmacies (dried).

茨實
MAKHANA

Makhana is the mature and dried seed kernel of a plant in the water lily family. It is steamed and processed with salt and is mainly produced in Zhaoqing, a prefecture in Guangdong, China. Makhana invigorates the spleen and removes dampness. In turn, it strengthens the kidneys and its essence. Cooked makhana is perfect for people who have a weak spleen or kidneys and frequent night urination.

WHERE TO BUY: Chinese supermarkets, herbal pharmacies.

羅漢果
MONK FRUIT

Mainly grown in Guangxi and less prevalently in southern China, monk fruit is rich in vitamin C, glycosides, fructose, glucose, and protein. It can treat acute and chronic bronchitis, pharyngitis, bronchial asthma, whooping cough, stomach fever, constipation, and acute tonsillitis.

The herb is good for clearing the heat and moisturizing the lungs. In recent years, monk fruit has gained a big following as a popular sweetener in the Western health food world.

WHERE TO BUY: Chinese herbal pharmacies.

鷓鴣
PARTRIDGE

The partridge is a bird native to Bangladesh, Bhutan, China, India, Laos, Myanmar, Nepal, Thailand, and Vietnam. Their meat is effective in removing phlegm in the lungs. Partridge is warm in nature and has high nutritional value. The broth made from partridge is a wonderful tonic for the body that can treat anemia and eliminate eye fatigue, improve general metabolism, prevent rheumatism, and alleviate nerve pain.

WHERE TO BUY: Special Chinese poultry markets.

玉竹
POLYGONATUM

Polygonatum, or jade bamboo, is good at nourishing yin energy and moisturizing the system, quenching the body's thirst, and stimulating the secretion of body fluids. The perennial plant also helps heal coughs caused by heat or dryness from the weather and strengthens the lungs and stomach. It is grown in northeastern China, Southeast Asia, and warm areas in Europe.

WHERE TO BUY: Chinese herbal pharmacies.

茯苓
PORIA MUSHROOM

Poria is a wood-decay fungus that tends to grow underground. It can be found in southwestern China. The mushroom has many functions, including clearing dampness, improving memory, strengthening the spleen, facilitating better urination, and calming nerves. It is also very helpful for patients with diarrhea. In lab tests with mice, poria was found to have anticancer qualities and the power to jump-start the immune system.

Poria is known as the "four seasons magic medicine" because it has a wide range of effects and can be used in all seasons. It is healthy and delicious and makes for great dishes. Since the mushroom improves urination, individuals who suffer from urination frequency issues should take it in moderation. Never consume poria with vinegar or strong tea, as the fungus may cause stomachaches or rashes.

WHERE TO BUY: Chinese herbal pharmacies.

紅棗
RED DATES (JUJUBE)

Jujube, also known as red dates, nourishes the body's overall energy and strengthens qi. It is good for the heart, lungs, spleen, stomach, and blood and helps soothe the nerves. The fruit is used for stimulating appetite and healing chronic diarrhea and anemia. Jujube is native to southern Asia but is popular around the world.

Jujube is considered a slightly hot food, so people with hot body types should eat the dates only in moderation. In soup, the pits should be taken out for hot body types. Since jujube contains high levels of sugar, people with diabetes should eat it selectively.

WHERE TO BUY: Chinese supermarkets, herbal pharmacies.

赤靈芝
RED LINGZHI (REISHI MUSHROOM)

Lingzhi has been revered in Asia for over two thousand years as the "mushroom of immortality." They improve blood circulation to the brain, lower blood sugar, protect the liver, and suppress tumor and cancer growth. The fungus is also known to improve the immune system and memory. In the wild, it grows at the base of the stumps of deciduous trees in China and North America.

WHERE TO BUY: Chinese herbal pharmacies.

茅根
RHIZOMA IMPERATAE

Rhizoma imperatae cools the blood to stop bleeding, clears stomach heat, and encourages urination. The herb can be used for stomach discomfort, lung heat, bitter taste in the mouth, thirst, and gum bleeding. Imperatae also removes dampness and detoxifies. It is a cold food, so cold bodies should avoid eating it or take it only in moderation during the summer. Imperatae grows in southern China and southeast Asia.

WHERE TO BUY: Chinese herbal pharmacies.

沙參
SAND GINSENG

Sand ginseng restores the lungs with yin qi, and invigorates and moisturizes the respiratory organ. The herb clears heat from both the lungs and stomach. It also regulates the immune system and strengthens heart functions. The root can be found in low mountain grasses and rock crevices, but also in grasslands at an altitude of 600 to 700 meters. There are two varieties: northern and southern sand ginseng.

WHERE TO BUY: Chinese herbal pharmacies.

海底椰
SEA COCONUT (DOUBLE COCONUT)

Sea coconut nourishes yin and moisturizes the lungs. It also removes dryness, clears heat, and relieves coughs. It belongs to the palm family and can be found in forests in the Ratchaburi region of Thailand.

WHERE TO BUY: Chinese herbal pharmacies.

雪梨
SNOW PEAR

Originally grown in central Europe and western Asia, snow pears are a magical fruit that resolves phlegm, moisturizes the lungs, and clears fire. The sweet treat is especially effective during the fall when the weather is dry. The important part of the pear is the skin, so boil the whole pear with the skin and drink the water. The skin is believed to be even more effective in relieving coughs and moisturizing the lungs.

Snow pears are slightly cold. Thus, cold body types should eat them in moderation. Those who have a cough that is cold in nature must avoid the fruit.

WHERE TO BUY: Chinese supermarkets.

竹蔗
SUGARCANE

Sugarcane is a grass used for sugar production. For that reason, it is the most popular plant in our guide! In TCM, the juice of the sugarcane is extracted from its stalks, or it can be eaten raw or dried. Sugarcane clears heat, promotes body fluid production, and moisturizes. It is suitable for summer heat dissipation and often is used in juice or soup for that purpose. Sugarcane can be found growing in southern China and Hunan, as well as many other parts of Asia.

WHERE TO BUY: Chinese supermarkets, herbal pharmacies.

陳皮

TANGERINE PEEL

Tangerine peels are the dried skins of mandarin oranges, made by peeling the citrus fruit and drying the skins in the sun before storing them away to age anywhere from several months to seventy years. The longer the peel is aged, the more it is prized for its medicinal properties. For this reason, buy them in Chinese establishments and do not attempt to make your own.

Some of the medicinal uses for tangerine peels include healing diarrhea, abdominal discomfort, and coughs. The skin also aids in the excretion of phlegm. Tangerine peels improve appetite during hot summers by stimulating the spleen and stomach.

WHERE TO BUY: Chinese supermarkets, herbal pharmacies.

土茯苓

TUCKAHOE

Tuckahoe is an herb with neutral properties. It removes dampness, strengthens the spleen and stomach, protects the liver, and improves toxic joints by assisting in their detoxification. The herb is mainly used for limb contracture—muscle and bone pain caused by syphilis and mercury poisoning. It grows in Hunan, Hubei, and Guangzhou in China.

WHERE TO BUY: Chinese herbal pharmacies, or occasionally Chinese supermarkets for fresh tuckahoe.

雪耳

WHITE SNOW FUNGUS

White snow fungus grows in tropical climates in Asia and North America on dead branches of broadleaf trees. It is a parasitic yeast that contains a great deal of carotene, which can tone the skin and stimulate the skin's metabolism—keeping it moist and tender and reducing wrinkles in the process. Snow fungus is rich in plant-based gelatin and contains 70 percent dietary fiber. Therefore it can promote gastrointestinal motility, improve constipation, and maintain intestinal health.

WHERE TO BUY: Chinese herbal pharmacies.

PART II

The **RECIPES**

Using Traditional Chinese Medicine as our base concept behind the soup formulations, we perceive the body as a whole machine. We have combined herbs in our recipes that complement different parts of the body so they will work together nicely. And obviously we adjusted the ingredients for taste too.

We often speak about herbs that are good for the spleen and the stomach. It's not that we care only about these two organs. When we eat, the food needs to be digested, then absorbed. Those are the important functions of the stomach (digestion) and the spleen (absorption). If they do not work well and in tandem, no matter how great the soup is, the nutrients will not be passed down to us. That is why these recipes always contain components that are good for the stomach and the spleen, as well as other nutritious ingredients for seasonal purposes—may it be for the spring to clear dampness or the summer to clear the heat.

The universe is a chain itself, as are the seasons as well. There is a Chinese saying about the human body: "Spring is the time to start, summer is the time for growth, fall is the time for harvesting, and winter is the time for storage."

We have to consider seasons as part of a harmonious network that interacts with each other instead of being independent of one another. They are the causes as well as the results of each other. During winter, if we do not conserve and store our body's energy properly, there won't be enough energy when spring arrives. Similarly, if spring does not start well, nothing will continue to grow well in the summer and the harvest will be poor in the fall. This is a great illustration of why we need to take our well-being seriously at all times in order to get the best results all year round.

Every Chinese herbal soup connoisseur must know the following things before boiling the soup:

1. Chinese soup making is measured in bowls of water; one bowl equals one cup.
2. The idea is to strain the soups and drink the broth. You can eat most of the ingredients, but never the herbs.
3. If a recipe calls for chicken, do not use the head and neck in the soup. That is commonly where birds receive shots, and those parts are considered toxic.
4. Do not drink the soups out of season. This can throw your body out of sync, the opposite of what you want to do.
5. Aside from the winter recipes, the soups in this book can be consumed more than once a week; we provide enough per season to give you variety, depending on your body type, yin and yang balance, how you're feeling that week, or what area you'd like to improve on.
6. Our recommended times for boiling the soup are approximations. Once your soup reaches its target volume as stated in the recipe, it's ready.
7. Any unconsumed broth made with meat can be kept in an airtight container for 24 hours in the refrigerator. Any vegetarian broth can be kept for 2 days.
8. The tips for each recipe help with purchasing the ingredients and preparing the soup. Be sure to read them!

CHAPTER

6

SPRING

pring is the time when plants start growing. The universe is filled with energy and the deadness of winter dissipates. As a result, the atmosphere is filled with yang qi (vivacious energy) as the land wakes up again.

People enjoy relaxed walks in meadows and parks to see the flowers blooming. At the same time, if our body is weakened from fatigue due to excess work or play, it is easy for us to catch a spring "cold," especially when our immune system is down, and an opportunity for our organs to trap the cold moisture from the air presents itself.

Spring air is filled with moisture. The weather is slightly cool and wet, with sunny and refreshing days in between. Spring rain brings humidity in the air that we absorb into our bodies. No matter what body type we are, we will experience this dampness, which causes the yang energy to be trapped inside us and unable to circulate and leads to discomfort and certain illnesses. This is especially true for people who are overweight or have weak immune systems.

Dampness gets trapped in our bodies for various reasons. One of the most common is eating fried and fatty food too frequently. Lack of exercise is another common reason. Spring should be the time to increase exercise and expel dampness out of our bodies. Avoid wearing wet clothes or letting your hair air-dry (which causes wetness around your head). If the humidity is high inside your home, consider buying a dehumidifier. Under these weather conditions, avoid eating sour food because the sourness can hurt your yang energy's growth.

The start of each season is a good time to retake your body quiz (see page 15) and reconfigure your yin and yang balance (see pages 21–22).

Those who are deficient in yang qi should use spring as the time to grow and store yang energy. Always keep yourself warmly clad, especially your back. Try to keep yourself in an uplifting mood and stay happy. This is the season to nurture your liver. If you come across unhappiness, make sure you find friends to talk through your problems.

During spring, it is especially important to go to sleep before 11:00 p.m. to give your liver the resting period it needs.

Our healing soups will prepare you against the weather changes associated with spring. The recipes use plants such as kapok tree flowers, rush pith, lotus seeds, and five-finger peach. We use fruits and vegetables like papayas, sweet potatoes, winter melons, figs, watercress, and artichokes.

The soups we introduce you to fit all body types with different body deficiency issues, as they are well balanced and neutral.

FIVE-FINGER PEACH, KUDZU ROOT, AND COIX SEED SOUP

SERVES 4

This soup is guaranteed to make your kitchen smell like flowers! The purpose of this fragrant broth is to remove dampness from your body and strengthen your spleen. This is wonderful for hot body types to drink and to prepare us for spring colds.

1. Rinse the kudzu root lightly. Place it in a container with just enough water to cover the root and soak for 15 minutes. Discard the water. Soak the kudzu root in a new bowl of enough water to cover for 2 hours.

2. Lightly rinse the other ingredients.

3. Place all of the ingredients into a pot, including the kudzu root with its soaking water. Add 7 cups of water. Bring the water to a boil over high heat, then turn the heat to low.

4. Simmer the soup for 2 hours, until reduced to slightly more than 4 cups.

5. Add salt, as desired, and enjoy.

16 ounces fresh kudzu root or 5 ounces dried kudzu root 粉葛

3 ounces five-finger peach 五指毛桃

1 ounce dried, roasted coix seeds 薏米 (熟)

3 frozen dried and peeled figs 無花果

14 ounces lean pork (optional)

8 cups water

Salt, for serving

TIPS

You can eat the figs and the pork but not the herbs.

Fresh kudzu root is hard to find, but dried kudzu root is readily available in Chinese supermarkets and herbal stores.

For dried coix seeds, try to buy the slightly roasted "ripe" coix seeds. If you can't find the roasted kind, you can purchase raw coix seeds. Put them in a pan and stir-fry them on low heat for 3 minutes. Do not use oil.

Use white figs, not the dark brown ones traditionally used for snacking. You can find white figs in the frozen section of Chinese herbal stores.

CHAYOTE, CHINESE YAM, LOTUS SEED, AND MAKHANA FISH SOUP

2 ounces dried Chinese yam 淮山

2 chayotes 合掌瓜

1 ounce dried lotus seeds 蓮子

2 small pieces dried tangerine peel 陳皮

1 ounce dried makhana 茨實

8 cups of water

1 small whole fish, preferably cod

1 tablespoon of vegetable oil

3 thin slices fresh ginger

Salt, for serving

This fish soup helps to improve the body's strength and expels dampness. Chinese yam strengthens the spleen and aids in the stomach's digestion. Lotus seeds are good for your heart and soothing your spirit. Tangerine peel improves qi, removes phlegm, and clears dampness. Makhana is beneficial for the kidneys.

1. Soak the Chinese yam in just enough water to cover it for 2 hours before making the soup. This water will be used as part of the total water needed to cook the soup.

2. Rinse the chayotes and cut them into cubes. No need to peel the skin away.

3. Rinse the lotus seeds, tangerine peels, and makhana.

4. Boil 1 cup of water and set it aside.

5. Rinse the fish, and discard its intestines.

6. Heat the oil in a pot over medium heat. Place the fish in the pot and lightly fry each side for 5 minutes.

7. Pour the reserved bowl of hot water into the pan. Steam will rise up.

8. Turn the heat to low. Pour in the rest of the ingredients and water. Simmer for 1½ hours, until the broth is reduced to 4 cups.

9. Stir salt to taste into the soup 10 minutes before serving.

TIPS

Fish soup is supposed to be white in color. To ensure that this happens, you must add hot water *after* you fry the fish. If you use room-temperature water, the soup will be clear and will not be as flavorful.

Use fish that has white flesh only. Stay away from tuna (red) and salmon (orange). Avoid fish with no scales, like catfish. Go for fish with larger and fewer bones.

When buying lotus seeds, the kind with the skin on is always preferable to the skinless ones.

Do not eat the herbs. You can eat the fish and lotus seeds.

POLYGONATUM, PAPAYA, COIX SEED, AND CHINESE YAM SOUP

Polygonatum is rich in vitamin A and niacin and works wonders for the skin. It has anti-aging properties, boosts the immune system, improves qi, and is an antioxidant. Coix seeds are effective in driving away dampness in the body during spring. Papaya is good for moisturizing the system, aids in digestion, and improves immunity. Chinese yam is good for the stomach. Together, these ingredients clear dampness and boost your immune system. This particular formulation is easy for the stomach to digest; just don't eat the herbs.

2 ounces Chinese yam (fresh or dried) 淮山

1 papaya

1 ounce dried, roasted coix seeds 薏米 (熟)

1 ounce raw, dried coix seeds 薏米 (生)

1 ounce polygonatum (jade bamboo) 玉竹

14 ounces lean pork

10 cups water

Salt, for serving

1. Two hours before making the soup, soak the Chinese yam in enough water to cover it. You will be using this water in the soup later.

2. Peel the papaya and cut up into medium-size pieces.

3. Rinse the coix seeds and polygonatum. Lightly rinse the pork.

4. Place all of the ingredients in a large pot with the 10 cups of water plus the water the yam was soaked in.

5. Bring the soup to a boil over high heat.

6. Turn the heat down to medium and let simmer for 1½ hours until the soup is reduced to 4 or 5 cups.

7. Add salt, as desired, 15 minutes before the soup is ready. Stir well before serving.

TIPS

Raw and roasted coix seeds look very similar in the store, so read the package carefully and ask the clerk for help if you are confused.

If you can't find roasted coix seeds, you can roast them yourself. Put the raw coix seeds in a pan and stir-fry them on low heat for 3 minutes. Do not use oil or water. If the seeds roast before the 3-minute mark, remove them from the stove earlier.

You can eat everything except the herbs.

SWEDE, CARROT, AND PORK SOUP

1 pound swede
(rutabaga)

1 pound carrots

2 ounces hyacinth beans
扁豆

1 ear of corn (with the
husk on)

14 ounces lean pork

6 honey dates 蜜棗

10 cups of water

Salt, for serving

Swede, carrots, and hyacinth beans are all rich in vitamin B. The beans excel at dispelling dampness and help the kidneys to detox. Corn is a nutritious food that helps to clear heat and moisturize. Although carrots and swede are cold foods, the other components in this recipe will soften their coldness. In TCM, corn (with the husk on) has been proven to strengthen the pancreas, which can help lower blood sugar in people with diabetes. Overall, this nutritious broth helps to clear dampness and promote better digestion.

1. Rinse and peel the swede and carrots. Chop into medium pieces.

2. Lightly rinse the hyacinth beans, corn (with the husk on), and pork.

3. Place all of the ingredients into a pot. Bring to a boil over high heat until the soup boils. Then turn down the heat and simmer for another 1½ hours until reduced to 4 cups.

4. Add salt, as desired, 15 minutes before serving.

TIPS

For cold body types, add 3 slices of fresh ginger to the soup.

If corn in the husk is not available, you can use bare corn on the cob. You can also use frozen corn on the cob, but do not use canned corn or bagged corn from the frozen section.

All of the ingredients (except for the corn husk) are edible.

WINTER MELON SOUP WITH PORK AND KAPOK TREE FLOWERS

SERVES 4 TO 5

Winter melon is a popular ingredient for Chinese soups. The vegetable is a fabulous source of vitamin C and good for blood vessels in the heart. Winter melons also clear heat out of the body. Kapok flowers, hyacinth beans, and adzuki beans are well known for their abilities to expel dampness. Figs moisturize the body, and lily leaves add a refreshing flavor to the soup while simultaneously helping the body to detox.

1. Cut the winter melon into 5 pieces. Discard the seeds but reserve the inner core and skin.

2. Lightly rinse the other ingredients. Use your hands to tear the lily leaf apart into 4 to 5 pieces.

3. Cut up the pork into smaller pieces and set aside.

4. Place the water in a pot and add all the other ingredients.

5. Bring to a boil over high heat. Then lower the heat to medium or low and simmer for another 2 hours, until reduced to 4 to 5 cups.

6. Add salt, to taste, 15 minutes before serving.

1/2 winter melon (approximately 2 pounds)

1 big lily leaf 荷葉

14 ounces lean pork

8 cups water

5 dried kapok tree flowers 木綿花

2 ounces adzuki beans 赤小豆

1 tangerine peel 陳皮

2 ounces hyacinth beans 扁豆

3 frozen dried and peeled figs 無花果

Salt, for serving

TIPS

We prefer to use winter melons that are dark green in color. There are lighter varieties available with hues similar to a green apple.

Use white figs, not the dark brown ones traditionally used for snacking. You can find white figs in the frozen section of Chinese herbal stores.

Do not eat the herbs.

SWEET POTATO WITH PAPAYA, SOYBEAN, AND FIG SOUP

12 ounces sweet potatoes

1 pound papaya

6 frozen dried and peeled figs 無花果

1 ounce sweet apricot kernels 南杏

1/2 ounce bitter apricot kernels 北杏

2 ounces soybeans 黃豆

14 ounces lean pork

10 cups water

This is a delightful broth that is light and nourishing. Sweet potatoes are a great source of beta-carotene, fiber, potassium, and vitamin C. They promote gut health, provide lubrication for joints, and improve immunity. Papaya improves digestion and supports the immune system. Combined with figs, apricot kernels, and soybeans, this soup provides good nutritional value, moisturizes and clears the system, and promotes good absorption by the body.

1. Peel the sweet potatoes and papaya, and cut them into medium-size pieces.

2. Lightly wash the figs, both kinds of apricot kernels, and soybeans.

3. Place all of the ingredients and the water in a pot, and bring to a boil over high heat.

4. Turn the heat down to medium and simmer for 1½ hours, or until the soup is reduced to 4 to 5 cups.

TIPS

Sweet potatoes and yams are often mislabeled or confused for one another at the grocery store. To be clear, we are referring to sweet potatoes that have red skins and orange flesh.

Use white figs, not the dark brown ones traditionally used for snacking. You can find white figs in the frozen section of Chinese herbal stores.

Do not eat the apricot kernels.

WATERCRESS SOUP WITH APRICOT KERNELS, PORK, LOTUS SEEDS, CHINESE YAM, AND MAKHANA

SERVES 4

This soup is a great way to get your greens! Watercress contains a lot of essential minerals, vitamins, and carotenoids, such as lutein and beta-carotene, both of which maintain eye and skin health. The leafy vegetable also clarifies and moisturizes the lungs, expels phlegm, and improves urination. Honey dates improve the flavor of the soup and help to reduce the cold nature of watercress.

1 pound watercress

1 teaspoon salt, plus more for serving

2 ounces Chinese yam (fresh or dried) 淮山

1 ounce sweet apricot kernels 南杏

1 ounce dried lotus seeds 蓮子

1 ounce makhana 茨實

14 ounces lean pork

2 honey dates 蜜棗

8 cups water

1. Wash the watercress in water twice. Then soak the watercress in water to cover. Add the salt and let sit for 20 minutes. Rinse thoroughly and set aside. Discard the water.

2. Lightly rinse the Chinese yam. Soak in just enough water to cover for 2 hours before boiling the soup. This water will be used as part of the total water needed to make the soup.

3. Lightly wash all of the other ingredients except the dates.

4. Place the water and all ingredients—except the watercress—in a pot. Bring to a boil over high heat and then add the watercress. (Adding the watercress too early can make the soup bitter.)

5. Turn the heat down to medium or low and simmer for 1 hour, or until the broth is reduced to 4 cups.

6. Add salt, as desired, 15 minutes before the broth is done.

TIPS

Since watercress is slightly on the cold side, people who are pregnant or have cold bodies should add 3 slices of fresh ginger to the soup.

Lotus seeds with the skin on are preferable to the skinless kind because they are slightly more nutritious.

Do not eat the herbs.

PORK SPLEEN, LILY BULB, COMMON RUSH, CHINESE YAM, AND DRIED TANGERINE PEEL SOUP

SERVES 4

This recipe removes dampness and refreshes the body. Lily bulbs are good for clearing heat from the lungs. Rush pith is known for quenching thirst, getting rid of dampness, and removing the heat (fire) that results from insufficient sleep. Tangerine peel improves qi and expels dampness.

1. Lightly rinse the Chinese yam. Place in a bowl with just enough water to cover, and soak for 2 hours before use. The water will be used as part of the total water needed to cook the soup.

2. Lightly rinse the lily bulbs, common rush, and tangerine peel. Soak the lily bulbs and common rush for 20 minutes before use.

3. Rinse the pork spleen. Cut away the skin and membrane (the clear part that wraps the spleen). Boil the spleen in 2 cups water for 5 minutes. Remove the spleen and discard the water. Rinse the spleen with cold tap water to remove any other impurities that may have surfaced.

4. Place all of the ingredients and remaining water in a pot. Bring to a boil over high heat. Turn the heat to medium-low and cook for 1½ to 2 hours, or until reduced to 3 cups.

5. Add salt, as desired, 15 minutes before serving.

2 ounces Chinese yam (fresh or dried) 淮山

2 ounces dried lily bulbs (fresh or dried) 百合

2 ounces common rush 灯芯花

1 tangerine peel 陳皮

1 pork spleen

14 ounces lean pork

3 thin slices fresh ginger

10 cups water

Salt, for serving

TIPS

You can find pork spleen at a Chinese supermarket.

If you can find fresh lily bulbs (note that they have become increasingly difficult to purchase), buy them instead of dried ones. The fresh kind can be found in the refrigerated section of Chinese grocery stores.

Do not eat the herbs.

ARTICHOKE SOUP WITH PORK AND APRICOT KERNELS

SERVES 4

1 big artichoke or
2 small artichokes

14 ounces lean pork

1 ounce sweet apricot
kernels 南杏

8 cups water

Salt, for serving

Artichokes are one of the few vegetables known for keeping the liver healthy. Two antioxidants found in artichokes—cynarine and silymarin—can effectively reduce the presence of toxins and facilitate their elimination from the liver and the body. Artichokes are high in fiber and loaded with vitamins and minerals such as vitamin C, vitamin K, folate, phosphorus, and magnesium. In TCM, it is believed that if the liver is healthy, the blood will be healthy, and, in turn, the qi will be good because healthy blood promotes qi growth. It is further believed that if the blood is clean and rid of toxins, the skin will be clear, glowing, and radiant. This is more than a healthy soup; it's a beauty soup! It's also a very simple soup to make.

1. Clean the artichoke thoroughly with a toothbrush and rinse with water. There is no need to cut up the artichoke.

2. Lightly rinse the pork and apricot kernels.

3. Place the water and all of the ingredients in a pot. Bring to a boil over high heat.

4. Lower the heat to medium-low and simmer for 1½ hours, or until reduced to 4 cups of broth and the artichoke is breaking down.

5. Add salt, as desired, 15 minutes before straining the soup. Discard all of the ingredients and enjoy the broth.

TIPS

Since you are not clipping the artichokes, be careful when you wash them because the edges are sharp.

You'll know the artichokes are done when the flower dismantles.

Drink the broth. Avoid eating the ingredients, especially the artichokes.

KUDZU ROOT, BEAN, DATE, AND PORK SOUP

SERVES 4

This is one of the most popular spring soups in Cantonese cooking. Generally all beans are excellent at driving away dampness. Kudzu root is extremely effective at clearing heat and lowering fire, lifting yin energy, and promoting body fluid production. It is believed that the active ingredients in kudzu root moisturize the skin and increase elasticity, in addition to having anti-aging properties. And if that isn't enough, kudzu root also lowers blood pressure and evens out blood sugar levels.

1. Lightly rinse the kudzu root. Place in a container and soak in water to cover for 15 minutes. Discard the water. Place the kudzu root in 1 cup fresh water and soak for 2 hours.

2. Lightly rinse the other ingredients.

3. Rinse the pork and cut into small pieces. In a pot, blanch the pork in boiling water for 5 minutes, until the impurities rise to the surface. Discard the water and set the pork aside. Rinse out the pot.

4. Add all the ingredients to the pot, including the kudzu root and the kudzu root soaking water. Add the 7 remaining cups of water. Bring the soup to a boil over high heat.

5. Turn the heat down to medium-low and simmer for 1½ hours, or until the broth is reduced to 4 cups.

6. Add salt, as desired, 15 minutes before serving. Strain and discard the ingredients before enjoying the broth.

2 pounds kudzu root (6 ounces if dried) 粉葛

14 ounces lean pork

2 ounces adzuki beans 赤小豆

2 ounces black-eyed peas 眉豆

2 honey dates 蜜棗

8 cups water

Salt, for serving

TIPS

Fresh kudzu roots are hard to find in Chinese grocery stores. However, if you live in the southern United States, you may be able to find them at local Western markets.

Just drink the soup. No need to eat the ingredients, which will not be very tasty after the boiling process.

CHAPTER

7

SUMMER

RECIPES

ummer air is filled with heat.

Prolonged exposure to summer heat causes strokes, headaches, and flus. Exercising in the summer results in sweat. Although sweat helps to relieve the heat in the body, thirst and heat persist on the skin.

An effective summer soup drives out the excessive heat that is still trapped in the body. This is especially important for people who do not exercise.

Ingredients like winter melon, lily leaves, dried sugarcane, and rhizoma imperatae are excellent at driving out summer heat. We also use plants like adzuki beans, black-eyed peas, apricot kernels, and honeysuckle. The soups also feature fruits and vegetables like old cucumbers, apples, water chestnuts, and parsley.

You may notice that some herbs that we use to expel dampness are often included in the summer soups. A certain amount of dampness is present in perspiration. These herbs will help the body get rid of any excessive dampness that remains.

PAPAYA, JUJUBE, AND DRIED BEAN CURD SOUP

SERVES 4

This is one of the sweeter-tasting broths in this chapter. Bean curd is known to clear summer heat, papaya is rich in vitamins and is highly nutritious, and jujube improves the blood and qi. Together, they make a light, refreshing, and great soup.

2 ounces dried bean curd strips 支竹 or sheets 腐竹片

11/2 pounds papaya

1 ounce sweet apricot kernels 南杏

8 jujube 紅棗

1 slice fresh ginger

8 cups water

Salt, for serving

1. Soak the bean curd strips in just enough water to cover for 1 hour. When the strips are softened, cut them into smaller strips and set aside. Discard the water.

2. Rinse and peel the papaya. Cut up into medium-size pieces and discard the seeds.

3. Lightly rinse the other ingredients.

4. Bring the water to a boil in a pot over high heat. Add all the ingredients except the bean curd strips, and cook for 1 hour, or until the broth reduces to 4 cups.

5. Add the bean curd strips and continue boiling for another 30 minutes.

6. Stir in salt, as desired, 15 minutes before serving. Discard the apricot kernels.

TIPS

Dried bean curd is sold in sheets and in strip-like pieces. Both are readily available in Asian supermarkets.

APRICOT KERNEL, APPLE, AND TOFU SOUP

SERVES 2

1 large or 2 small apples

1 14-ounce carton firm tofu

4 cups plus 3 ounces water

1 ounce pickled cabbage

1 ounce sweet apricot kernels 南杏

3 ounces cornstarch

Salt and sesame oil, for serving

This is another simple and easy soup to make. Both apples and tofu are nutritious, and tofu, like all other soybean products, is good for clearing heat from your body. This soup also refreshes your mind, quenches your thirst, promotes saliva secretion, and improves urination.

1. Peel and core the apples, and cut up into bite-size pieces.

2. Cut the tofu into bite-size pieces.

3. Bring 4 cups of water to a boil over high heat. Add the apples, tofu, cabbage, and apricot kernels, and turn the heat down to low. Cook for 45 minutes, or until the broth reduces to 2 cups.

4. In a separate bowl, stir the cornstarch with 3 ounces water. Mix well until the cornstarch is fully dissolved and there are no clumps. Pour into the soup and stir well.

5. Discard the apricot kernels.

6. Add salt, as desired, and a few drops of sesame oil to the soup right before serving.

TIPS

Pickled cabbage can be found in the frozen food section of Chinese supermarkets. You can also find pickled cabbage that is canned, but it has more preservatives and is not our preference.

You can eat all the ingredients except the apricot kernels.

Healing Herbal Soups

DRIED GINKGO NUT, BEAN CURD, AND LILY BULB SOUP

This is an effective soup that clears the summer heat from the body and strengthens the lungs at the same time. Ginkgo nuts smooth blood vessels, improve brain function, delay aging, and improve blood supply to the brain. They are also believed to protect the liver. Soybeans, a slightly "cool" food, expel the heat and are rich in isoflavones, unsaturated fatty acids, and cellulose, which can reduce cardiovascular disease and have the effect of lowering blood lipids. They are rich in calcium and can alleviate the symptoms associated with menopause.

1. Remove the ginkgo nuts from their shells, and soak the nuts in a small bowl of water. When the skin is soft, remove it, discard the water, and set the nuts aside.

2. Lightly fry the soybeans with a little water in a saucepan or wok. This will help the soybeans be less "cool."

3. Lightly rinse the lily bulbs.

4. If using the pork, rinse and cut into small pieces. In a pot, blanch the pork in boiling water for 5 minutes, until the impurities rise to the surface. Discard the water, and set the pork aside. Rinse out the pot.

5. Bring the 12 cups water to a boil in the pot over high heat. Add in all of the ingredients, and lower the heat to medium-low. Simmer for 1½ hours, or until the broth reduces to 5 cups. If using the pork stomach, simmer for 2 hours.

6. Stir in salt, as desired, 15 minutes before the soup is ready. Discard the gingko nuts before serving.

2 teaspoons ginkgo nuts 银杏

2 ounces soybeans 黄豆

2 ounces lily bulbs (fresh or dried) 百合

12 cups water

14 ounces lean pork or one pork stomach (optional)

2 dried bean curd sheets

2 slices fresh ginger

Salt, for serving

TIPS

Do not eat the ginkgo nuts raw because they are slightly toxic. They must be cooked for eating. Children under ten years of age should not eat them at all. To be on the safe side and because of the bitter taste, we recommend discarding the ginkgo nuts before drinking this broth. You can enjoy the other ingredients.

DUCK with CHING PO LEUNG SOUP

1/2 wild duck (teal)
(about 1 1/2 pounds) 水鴨

2 jujube 紅棗

3 thin slices fresh
ginger

8 cups water

1 package
Ching Po Leung 清补凉,
which contains
1 ounce each of:

Chinese yam 淮山

Lotus seeds 蓮子

Makhana 茨實

Polygonatum 玉竹

Adenophora stricta 沙參

Lily bulb 百合

Coix seeds 薏米

Longan fruit 桂圓肉

Sweet apricot kernels 南杏

Heavy tonics are not advised during the summer because the high temperatures can cause us to feel dry and hot, and we end up perspiring heavily. That is why it is important to pick a gentle, moisturizing soup that helps replenish our system while simultaneously removing heat and dryness. A popular all-purpose tonic soup is Ching Po Leung, an herbal broth. "Ching" in Chinese means clear, "po" means tonic, and "leung" means cooling. With a special combination of dried herbs, Ching Po Leung is widely used in Cantonese households as a soup base in the summer. You can find it ready-made in packages at the Chinese supermarket.

Teal (or wild duck) is a slightly cold food, but adding ginger neutralizes it. Teal improves qi, reduces swelling, and detoxifies. It can warm the body, strengthen the liver, and replenish yin deficiency.

1. Clean and wash the teal.

2. Bring enough water to cover the teal and bring to a boil over high heat. Add the teal and cook for 10 minutes. Discard the water and set the teal aside.

3. Lightly rinse the jujube and all the ingredients in the Ching Po Leung package.

4. Place all of the ingredients, including the teal and water, in a pot. Bring to a boil over high heat. Then turn the heat down to medium-low and cook for 2 hours, until reduced to 4 cups.

5. Discard all of the ingredients except the duck, if desired, and enjoy.

TIPS

Do not drink this soup if you have a cold or flu as it may worsen your condition.

Teal is available at Chinese poultry shops.

Ching Po Leung is available in small packages at Chinese supermarkets or herbal stores. There are many variations of Ching Po Leung. Some use six different herbs, and some include up to ten. Any variation works. We prefer the ingredient combination stated in the recipe, but if you can't find that particular variation, that is fine.

You can eat the duck but not the rest of the ingredients.

CARROT, WATER CHESTNUT, AND PORK SOUP

SERVES 4

This is a sweet, refreshing, and delicious soup and one of the most accessible in this chapter because it requires *no Chinese herbs*! Carrots are rich in vitamin A and beta-carotene. Water chestnuts are good for clearing heat in the summer and removing phlegm in the system. Corn strengthens the spleen and stomach. When cooked with the husk and silk, corn is extremely beneficial for the pancreas and a wonderful food for people with diabetes. These three ingredients are combined with pork shank to create a soup that clears heat and toxins, quenches thirst, nourishes yin, and promotes body fluid production, all while invigorating the spleen.

4 carrots

3 ears of corn

6 water chestnuts

14 ounces pork shank

8 cups water

Salt, for serving

1. Wash and peel the carrots. Cut into big pieces.

2. Wash the corn. If possible, keep the husk and corn silk. Cut each ear of corn into a few pieces.

3. Wash and peel the water chestnuts. Cut each in half.

4. Wash the pork shank. Bring enough water to cover it to a boil in a pot. Add the pork shank, and boil for 5 minutes. Discard the water, and set the pork aside. Rinse out the pot.

5. Place all ingredients and the 8 cups of water in the pot. Bring to a boil over high heat. Then lower the heat to medium-low and simmer for 1½ hours, until reduced to 4 cups.

6. Stir in salt, as desired.

TIPS

If you cannot find corn with the husk and silk intact, you can use corn without them, although that's less preferable.

You can eat all the ingredients in this soup.

ADZUKI BEAN, BLACK-EYED PEA, OLD CUCUMBER, AND CARROT SOUP

SERVES 4

1 old cucumber

1 carrot

2 ounces adzuki beans
赤小豆

2 ounces black-eyed
peas 眉豆

3 scallops

14 ounces pork shank

3 honey dates 蜜棗

3 thin slices fresh
ginger

1 tangerine peel 陳皮

8 cups water

Salt, for serving

This very popular soup in Chinese households is used to clear out heat in the body. Old cucumber, as the name suggests, is a very ripe cucumber. As cucumber ages, its skin turns yellowish brown. The vegetable is rich in vitamins A, B6, C, and E and is believed to have anti-aging effects. Old cucumbers, which are sometimes called baby yellow gourds, contain lots of fiber, so they also help with improving bowel movements, lowering cholesterol, and detoxing. TCM believes that old cucumbers increase yin energy.

Carrots improve our immunity and contain beta-carotene. Carrots, adzuki beans, and black-eyed peas are a well-known trifecta for removing dampness. Honey dates moisturize the system, while tangerine peel improves qi and gets rid of dampness as well.

1. Rinse the old cucumber, and scrape out the seeds and the core. Leave the skin on. Cut the cucumber into medium pieces and set aside.

2. Peel the carrot; then wash it and cut into medium pieces.

3. Rinse the remaining ingredients except the honey dates. Set all of these aside.

4. Bring 2 cups water to a boil in a pot over high heat. Add the pork shank and boil for 5 minutes. Discard the water.

5. Place all of the ingredients and the remaining 6 cups of water in the pot. Bring to a boil over high heat. Turn the heat to low and simmer for 1½ hours, until reduced to 4 cups.

6. Stir in salt, as desired, 15 minutes before the soup is ready. Discard the adzuki beans, tangerine peel, and black-eyed peas before serving.

TIPS

For a lighter meal, make this a vegetable soup by omitting the scallops and pork and adding a few mushrooms, preferably shiitake.

Do not eat the adzuki beans, tangerine peel, and black-eyed peas. They are hard to digest.

FISH with TOFU and PARSLEY SOUP

SERVES 4

Fish is a great neutral food, which makes it suitable for everyone, including pregnant women and people who are ill. Fish is rich in protein, calcium, and all kinds of vitamins that can easily be absorbed. Tofu is made from soybeans and is rich in nutrients, such as iron, calcium, phosphorus, and magnesium. A slightly cool food, tofu also contains rich high-quality protein and essential amino acids. It can nourish the qi, clear heat and moisturize, promote body fluid production, quench thirst, and clean the stomach. Tofu is especially beneficial for people with hot body types.

11/2 pounds cod

1 12-ounce package tofu

2 or 3 sprigs fresh parsley

1 spring onion

8 cups water

Vegetable oil, for frying

2 thin slices fresh ginger

Salt and freshly ground black pepper

1. Remove the fish intestines. Rinse the inside of the fish, and then rinse it all. Set aside.

2. Cut the tofu into small square pieces. Set aside.

3. Cut the parsley and spring onion (both white and green parts) into a few pieces. Separate the green portion of the onion from the white portion.

4. Bring the water to a boil over high heat.

5. Meanwhile, put a little oil in a pan. When hot, add the fish and lightly fry for 10 minutes, flipping halfway through.

6. Place the fish in the boiling water. Skim any white residue from the surface of the water after 5 minutes. Add the ginger, the white portion of the onion, and the tofu.

7. After 5 minutes, remove any remaining white residue from the top of the soup. Turn the heat to medium, and cook for 45 minutes, until the soup turns white and reduces to 4 cups.

8. Add the parsley and salt and pepper to taste 15 minutes before serving. Sprinkle the soup with the green portion of the onion and serve.

TIPS

TCM believes fish without scales are more toxic than ones with the scales. Try to buy white-fleshed fish with scales. For this soup, we suggest cod. Choose fish with larger and fewer bones.

You can eat all the ingredients in this soup, but beware of fish bones (obviously).

SUGARCANE, RHIZOMA IMPERATAE, AND WATER CHESTNUT DRINK

SERVES 5

This recipe is not for an actual soup; it's for a popular summer drink that is prepared like a soup. This formulation has a cooling effect on the body and fits any body type and any age. The drink, which can be served hot, at room temperature, or cold, also helps to strengthen qi, moisturize the system, and moisturize the skin. And like the soups that precede this recipe, this beverage expels heat.

1. Peel the skin off the sugarcane if using fresh. If using dried sugarcane, just lightly rinse.

2. Peel the carrots. Rinse lightly and cut into small pieces.

3. Peel the water chestnuts. Rinse and halve each water chestnut.

4. Put all of the ingredients in a pot, and bring to a boil over high heat.

5. Turn the heat down to low, and simmer for 1½ hours, until reduced to 5 cups.

6. Strain and enjoy.

1/2 pound fresh sugarcane or 6 ounces dried sugarcane (found in Chinese herbal stores)

2 ounces carrots

10 water chestnuts

1/2 ounce rhizoma imperatae 茅根

1 ounce dried honeysuckle flowers 金银花

10 cups water

TIPS

If you cannot finish the drink in one day, place it in an airtight container and refrigerate it. The drink stays fresh for 48 hours.

Do not eat the herbs. You can chew the sugarcane, but do not swallow it.

MUNG BEAN, WINTER MELON, LILY LEAF, AND LOTUS SEED SOUP

11/2 pounds winter melon

1 piece dried lily leaf 荷葉

2 teaspoons mung beans 綠豆

14 ounces lean pork

6 or 7 lotus seeds 蓮子

8 cups water

Salt, for serving

This is a refreshing and rejuvenating soup for the whole family to enjoy. Lily leaves and winter melons are essential in Chinese kitchens for clearing heat. When summer heat is trapped in our bodies, it creates dampness, and we perspire a lot and tire easily. This soup helps to dispel both the heat and the dampness. This broth is helpful in weight loss, too.

1. Rinse and cut open the winter melon. Discard the seeds and the core.

2. Lightly rinse the lily leaf, and tear it into smaller pieces. Soak the pieces in water for 5 minutes. Discard the water.

3. Lightly rinse the mung beans and pork. Cut the pork into 1-inch cubes.

4. Place all the ingredients in a pot with the water. Bring to a boil over high heat; then turn the heat down to low. Simmer for 1½ hours, until reduced to 3 to 4 cups.

5. Stir in salt, as desired, about 10 minutes before the soup is done. Discard the lily leaf before serving.

TIPS

Try to buy the dark green variety of winter melon. The lighter green is often a hybrid of another type of melon.

You can eat the winter melon with its skin and the lotus seeds, along with most of the other ingredients. However, do not eat lily leaves.

Purchase lotus seeds that come with the skin on. Only buy skinless ones if there is no other option.

FUZZY MELON, TEA TREE MUSHROOM, BLACK-EYED PEA, AND ADZUKI BEAN SOUP

SERVES 4

Adzuki beans and black-eyed peas are an indispensable pair for removing dampness. Fuzzy melon is high in vitamin C, fiber, and potassium. Tea tree mushrooms are an excellent wild fungus with special medicinal value. They enhance immunity, lower cholesterol, and are anti-aging. It is also believed that tea tree mushrooms can help kidney problems, such as frequent urination and bed-wetting in children. Overall, this soup strengthens the spleen and the kidneys and removes dampness from the body due to summer heat.

1. Remove the skin from the fuzzy melons by scraping it with a wide knife. Rinse the melon, and cut into smaller portions.

2. Soak the tea tree mushrooms, adzuki beans, black-eyed peas, and cashew nuts in water for 15 minutes. Rinse and set aside.

3. Lightly rinse the tangerine peel.

4. Bring the 6 cups of water to a boil in a pot over high heat. Add all of the ingredients. Turn the heat down to low and simmer for 1 hour, until reduced to 3 cups.

5. Add salt as desired, 10 minutes before it is done.

2 fuzzy melons 節瓜

2 ounces dried tea tree mushrooms 茶樹菇

2 ounces adzuki beans 赤小豆

2 ounces black-eyed peas 眉豆

2 teaspoons cashew nuts

1 tangerine peel 陳皮

6 cups water

Salt, for serving

TIPS

Technically you are not really peeling the fuzzy melon; you are scraping off the green part of the skin with a wide knife.

You can eat the melon and the mushrooms.

CHAPTER

8

FALL

RECIPES

s we shift into fall, there is less daylight and the days become shorter. In Traditional Chinese Medicine, this is an example of the slow swing from a time of yang to a time of yin. The foliage around you is a constant reminder of this. Leaves start falling, temperatures drop, the wind picks up into a crisp breeze, and the air becomes dry. Perhaps your body feels slightly uneasy at the growing aridness, as well as the transition from hot and humid to dry and windy. The change to fall is hard to adjust to, especially if your body is run-down.

No matter where you live, it is important to "moisturize" your organs against the drop in temperature and the dryness in the air. Our throat, lips, and nose are especially affected by this lack of moisture and may experience cracking. In this chapter, we teach you how to combat dryness with plants like goji berries, winter fungus, and monk fruit. Fruits like coconuts, figs, apples, and tangerine skins are also featured.

CROCODILE SOUP WITH CHINESE YAM AND MAKHANA

SERVES 5

At first glance, the rough, scaly exterior of crocodiles may not seem very appetizing. In Traditional Chinese Medicine, that is not the point: the aquatic reptiles are valued far more for their medicinal properties than for their taste. Crocodile meat is known for strengthening the lungs and qi. It also helps to remove phlegm in the lungs and provides relief to those with coughs and asthma. People with asthma, in particular, have a tough time weathering the summer-to-fall change because the airways have to adjust to the drop in temperatures and the dryness in the air. Together with Chinese yam and makhana, this soup improves qi overall, stabilizes yin energy, and moisturizes the lungs.

1. Rinse the crocodile meat, and cut it into medium pieces.

2. Place the crocodile in a pot with enough water to cover, add the ginger, and bring to a boil over high heat. After 5 minutes, remove the meat and set aside. Discard the water.

3. Lightly rinse the yam, makhana, apricot kernels, frozen figs, and tangerine peel.

4. Wash the lily bulbs and separate into petals.

5. Bring the 10 cups of water to a boil in the pot over high heat. Add the crocodile and all the other ingredients. Once the water starts boiling again, turn the heat down to medium-low and simmer for 1½ hours, until reduced to 5 cups.

6. Add salt to taste, 10 minutes before the soup is ready. Strain and discard all the ingredients except the crocodile meat, if desired.

14 ounces fresh crocodile meat or 8 ounces dried

3 thin slices fresh ginger

2 ounces Chinese yam (fresh or dried) 淮山

1 ounce makhana 茨實

1 ounce sweet apricot kernels 南杏

1/2 ounce bitter apricot kernels 北杏

4 frozen figs 無花果

1 tangerine peel

3 ounces lily bulbs (fresh or dried) 百合

10 cups water

Salt, for serving

TIPS

Crocodile meat is available at specialty poultry shops and occasionally at Chinese supermarkets, usually in the frozen foods section.

You can find dried figs in the frozen food section of Chinese supermarkets.

You can use fresh lily bulbs if you can find them in the frozen foods section of Chinese supermarkets. If not, a dried package of lily bulbs is fine to use. If you use dried lily bulbs, soak them in water to cover for 15 minutes. Discard the water before placing the lily bulbs in the soup with the other ingredients.

You can eat the meat after you drink the soup. Discard the other ingredients.

SEA COCONUT SOUP WITH CHESTNUTS AND FIGS

14 ounces boneless, skinless chicken breast

1 ounce dried sea coconut 海底椰

10 chestnuts

4 frozen figs 無花果

1 ounce sweet apricot kernels 南杏

1/2 ounce bitter apricot kernels 北杏

10 cups water

Salt, for serving

Sea coconut is moisturizing and good for clearing heat from the respiratory system. This type of heat is different from summer heat. Heat that is trapped in the lungs during fall is most commonly caused by pollution or ingesting the wrong things (such as drinking alcohol or eating very spicy or fried foods).

Chicken helps to improve our energy levels and blood supply. Chestnuts are nutritious in minerals and vitamins, especially vitamin C. They are also known to strengthen the elasticity of blood vessels. With the addition of apricot kernels and figs, this nutritious soup strengthens the body and boosts the immune system so that we can better weather the summer-to-fall transition.

1. Cut the chicken into medium pieces. Place in boiling water for 5 minutes. Pour out the water and set the chicken aside.

2. Lightly rinse the sea coconut. It should already be in thin slices if you bought the packaged version.

3. Remove the shells and skin from the chestnuts. Lightly rinse the chestnuts, figs, and apricot kernels.

4. Bring the 10 cups of water to a boil in a pot over high heat, and add all of the ingredients. Bring to a boil again; then turn the heat down to medium and simmer for 2 hours, until reduced to 5 cups.

5. Add salt to taste, about 10 minutes before the soup is ready. Strain the broth, and discard all the ingredients except the chicken and chestnuts, if desired.

TIPS

Sea coconuts are usually packaged dried and in slices at the Chinese grocery store.

If you cannot find fresh chestnuts, you can use dried chestnuts, which are available at Chinese supermarkets. If you use dried chestnuts, soak them in enough water to cover for 10 minutes before adding them to the soup. Discard the water when done.

You can eat the meat and chestnuts after you drink the soup, and discard the other ingredients.

COCONUT, GOJI BERRY, SNOW FUNGUS, AND JUJUBE SOUP SERVES 4

This is a nourishing, sweet, tasty soup for strengthening the lungs and boosting the overall immune system. Coconut is a great fruit to use for herbal broths because it is neutral and nutritious. It warms the body and replenishes the spleen and stomach while promoting body fluid secretion.

Snow fungus moisturizes the lungs and nourishes the skin, the stomach, and the kidneys. The gelatinous food increases yin energy and relieves coughs. Goji berries contain iron and help improve the blood supply. They also improve qi. Lotus seeds have a significant heart-strengthening effect, calm the nerves, and encourage better sleep.

1 large coconut

4 snow fungus 雪耳

6 dried shitake mushrooms

2 ounces Chinese yam (fresh or dried) 淮山

8 jujube 紅棗

1 ounce goji berries 枸杞

1 ounce lotus seeds 蓮子

8 cups water

Salt, for serving

1. Scoop the meat from the coconut and chop into small pieces. Rinse and set aside.

2. Lightly rinse the snow fungus. Soak in enough water to cover for 45 minutes. Tear the flower body from the core, and discard the core. Separate the flower body into small pieces. Set aside.

3. Rinse the dried mushrooms. Soak in water to cover for 20 minutes, or until softened. Remove the mushrooms and cut into smaller pieces. Discard the stems. Save the soaking water for cooking the soup. Set aside.

4. Lightly rinse the yam, jujube, goji berries, and lotus seeds. Set aside.

5. Bring the 8 cups of water and the mushroom soaking water to a boil in a pot over high heat. Add all of the ingredients, turn the heat down to low, and simmer for 1½ hours until reduced to 4 cups.

6. Add salt, as desired, 10 minutes before serving.

TIPS

When you buy snow fungus, choose the ones that are not too white. The very white snow fungus is often bleached, is of lower quality, and takes longer to soften. Opt for the beige-colored snow fungus because it is higher grade.

If you can't find fresh coconut, you can use shredded frozen coconut.

Add 4 ounces of skinless chicken breast for more flavor.

You can eat all the ingredients in this soup.

PIG SHANK, DRIED OYSTER, AND FUZZY MELON SOUP

SERVES 4

2 1/2 ounces dried oysters

1 tablespoon vegetable oil

1 slice fresh ginger

14 ounces lean pork

2 fuzzy melons 節瓜

2 ounces Chinese yam (fresh or dried) 淮山

8 cups water

3 honey dates 蜜棗

Salt, for serving

One of the downsides of autumn is that when the environment is dry, the "fire" in our body will start to accumulate, particularly if we spend one too many late nights at the office. The change in weather will make us feel "heated up," and we may find ourselves losing our temper easily. Dried oysters will help with lowering this heat by giving us better peace of mind.

Dried oysters are a nutritious food. They help to remove toxins from the body and improve the body's immunity. The magnesium in them speeds up metabolism, reduces oxidative stress, nourishes the skin, and improves liver function. Fuzzy melon reduces heat as well, and honey dates help to moisturize the system.

1. Place the oysters in a large bowl, and cover with hot water. Let soak for 20 minutes, until softened. Discard the water and set the oysters aside.

2. Heat the vegetable oil in a pot over medium heat and stir-fry the ginger. When the oil begins to sizzle, add the oysters. After a few minutes, remove the oysters, drain the oil, and set the oysters aside.

3. Rinse the pork, and cut into small pieces. In the pot, blanch the pork in boiling water for 5 minutes, until the impurities rise to the surface. Discard the water and set the pork aside. Rinse out the pot.

4. Scrape the skin off the fuzzy melons. Rinse and cut into small pieces.

5. Rinse the Chinese yam and set aside.

6. Bring the 8 cups of water to a boil in a pot over high heat. Add all of the ingredients, turn the heat down to low, and simmer for 1½ hours, until reduced to 4 cups.

7. Add salt, as desired, 10 minutes before the soup is ready. Discard the dates and enjoy.

TIPS

Dried oysters are available at Chinese supermarkets and herbal stores. Do not use fresh or canned oysters because they are "damp" foods.

You can eat all the ingredients in this soup except the dates, which will be tasteless by the end of boiling because all the flavor goes into the soup.

Healing Herbal Soups

APPLE, PEAR, FIG, PORK, AND TANGERINE PEEL SOUP

SERVES 4

All the soups for fall are focused on moisturizing our bodies and getting our system ready for the cold winter. Pears, apples, and figs—all neutral foods—are great for that purpose. Pears and figs are also well known in TCM for clearing heat and moisturizing and strengthening lungs. This soup will provide relief to the throats, respiratory system, and skin. Skin needs to be moisturized from the inside out in order for it to remain healthy and supple all year round.

3 red apples

3 snow pears (Chinese white pears) 雪梨

1 dried tangerine peel 陳皮

10 frozen figs 無花果

14 ounces lean pork

8 cups water

Salt, for serving

1. Peel the apples and pears. Cut into small pieces and set aside.

2. Lightly rinse the tangerine peel and the frozen figs. Set aside.

3. Rinse the pork and cut into small pieces. In a pot, blanch the pork in boiling water for 5 minutes, until the impurities rise to the surface. Discard the water and set the pork aside.

4. Rinse out the pot and bring the 8 cups of water to a boil over high heat and add the remaining ingredients. Turn the heat down to medium, and simmer for 1½ hours, until reduced to 4 cups.

5. Add salt to taste, 10 minutes before the soup is ready. Strain and discard all the ingredients except the apples and pears, if desired.

TIPS

Do not buy Asian pears, which have a brown skin and a round shape. Snow pears have yellow skin and are cone shaped.

Peel the apples if they are not organic. If they are organic, you can keep the skin on. The skin is actually very nutritious.

You can eat the apples and pears after you drink the soup.

PARTRIDGE, FRITILLARIA BULB, AND FIVE BEAN SOUP

1 to 2 partridges
(11/2 pounds total) 鷓鴣

1 teaspoon fritillaria
bulb 川貝

3 ounces black beans
黑豆

2 ounces black-eyed
peas 眉豆

1 ounce red beans 紅豆

2 ounces adzuki beans
赤小豆

1 ounce mung beans
綠豆

1 ounce dwarf lilyturf
麥冬

2 ounces dried lily bulb
百合

1 ounce coix seeds 薏米

10 cups water

Salt, for serving

In TCM, we believe different beans benefit different organs but that all beans nourish the system. Black beans are particularly good for invigorating the kidneys and improving their qi, promoting blood circulation, and dispelling all dryness caused by wind and weather. Red beans are rich in iron, promote qi, and strengthen the heart's functions. They are highly beneficial for the spleen and enhance digestion and absorption by the stomach. Partridge broth is an excellent tonic for the lungs as it removes phlegm and relieves coughs. Fritillaria bulb eradicates mucus and strengthens the lungs and is often used in herbal decoctions for cough relief and expelling phlegm.

1. Rinse the partridge. Discard the intestines, head, and neck. Cut the meat into small pieces.

2. Put the partridge pieces in a pot, cover with water, and bring to a boil. When white impurities from the meat float to the surface, turn off the heat. Set the partridge aside and discard the water.

3. Lightly rinse all the other ingredients. Set aside.

4. Bring the 10 cups of water to a boil in the pot over high heat. Add all of the ingredients, including the reserved partridge; turn the heat down to low; and simmer for 2 hours until reduced to 5 cups.

5. Add salt, as desired, 10 minutes before serving. Strain and enjoy the broth.

TIPS

Red beans are not the same as adzuki beans, although they do look similar. Red beans are round and usually bright red. Adzuki beans are longer and have a thin white line down the middle. Red beans are sweet, while adzuki beans taste plainer. Both are available at Chinese supermarkets and herbal stores.

Partridge is available at specialty poultry shops. Ask the butcher to remove the body parts you don't want to save you time.

If you are a cold body type, remember to lightly fry the coix seeds for about 3 minutes before adding them to the soup. Do not add oil to fry.

We recommend just drinking the soup and discarding the ingredients. The lily bulbs and partridge are edible, but the rest will be tasteless or hard to digest.

❀   **Healing Herbal Soups**

APRICOT KERNEL, BOK CHOY, HONEY DATE, AND PORK SOUP

SERVES 4

This is a basic soup for the fall, and the recipe for it is widely circulated among southern Chinese households. Honey dates and dried bok choy are known for moisturizing the body, while apricot kernels help to strengthen the lungs. The pork and the bok choy also help to make the soup heartier and more of a meal.

1. Lightly rinse the dried bok choy, then soak in enough water to cover for 1 hour. Drain and set aside.

2. Lightly rinse the apricot kernels.

3. Rinse the pork and cut into small pieces. In a pot, blanch the pork in boiling water for 5 minutes, until the impurities rise to the surface. Discard the water and set the pork aside. Rinse out the pot.

4. Bring the 8 cups of water to a boil in the pot over high heat. Add all the ingredients, lower the heat to medium, and cook for about 1½ hours, until reduced to 4 cups.

5. Add salt to taste, 10 minutes before the soup is ready. Strain and discard all the ingredients except the meat and bok choy, if desired.

11/2 6- to 8-ounce packages dried bok choy 白菜乾

1 ounce sweet apricot kernels 南杏

1/2 ounce bitter apricot kernels 北杏

14 ounces lean pork

8 cups water

4 honey dates 蜜棗

Salt, for serving

TIPS

You can use fresh bok choy instead of dried; just be sure to cook it a bit longer.

You can eat the meat and bok choy after you drink the soup.

MONK FRUIT, CHINESE YAM, CONCH, AND FIG SOUP

SERVES 4

1/2 ounce dwarf lilyturf
麥冬

2 ounces Chinese yam
(fresh or dried) 淮山

8 ounces fresh conch
meat or 5 ounces dried
響螺

1 monk fruit 羅漢果

4 frozen dry figs 無花果

1 tangerine peel 陳皮

8 cups water

Salt, for serving

This soup conserves fluids in the organs and improves skin texture. Conch, a cold food, provides good supplementary protein for the skin. It is great for maintaining and improving the body's immunity. Conch also invigorates the spleen and stomach and nourishes the blood, liver, and kidneys.

Monk fruit cures coughs and colds. It is often used to moisturize the lungs, remove phlegm, and clear heat and fire from the body. Dwarf lilyturf improves yin energy and increases the body's production of saliva and bodily fluids.

1. Lightly rinse the dwarf lilyturf and Chinese yam. Then soak in enough room-temperature water to cover for 4 hours.

2. If you are using fresh conch, wash it with some salt and scrub it. Then rinse and soak it in hot water for a couple of minutes. If you are using dried conch, lightly rinse and soak in enough room-temperature water to cover for 1 hour.

3. Lightly rinse the monk fruit. Break the shell up with your hands into smaller pieces. Set aside the shell pieces and the flesh.

4. Lightly rinse the frozen figs. Split each fig into half.

5. Soak the tangerine peel in water until softened. Clean the inner part of the peel to remove any residue.

6. Bring the 8 cups of water to a boil in a pot over high heat. Add all of the ingredients except the monk fruit, and simmer for 1 hour, until reduced to 4½ cups.

7. Add the monk fruit, and cook for another 20 minutes, until reduced to 4 cups.

8. Add salt as desired and cook for another 10 minutes. Strain before enjoying the broth.

TIPS

You can substitute the conch meat with the head of a conch, which is sold separately at Chinese herbal stores and supermarkets.

Drink only the soup. The conch, in particular, will harden after boiling, so it will be difficult to digest.

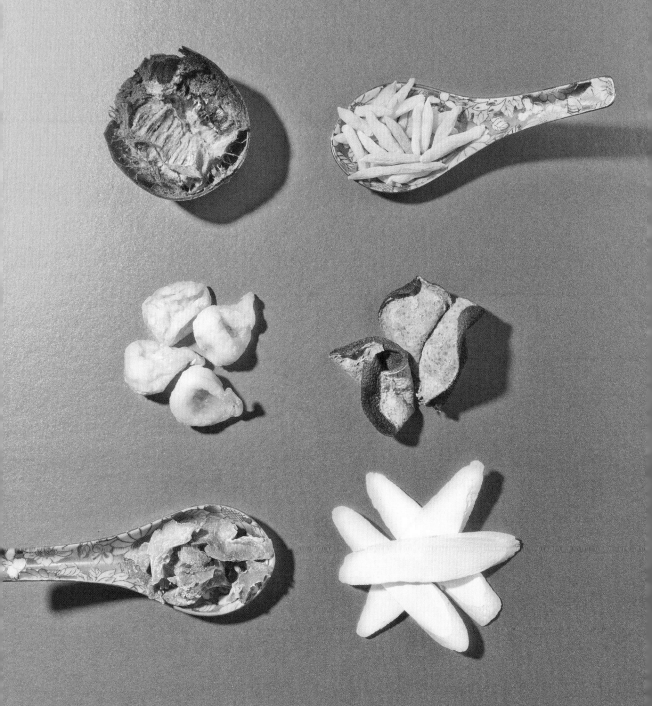

POLYGONATUM, SAND GINSENG, WATER CHESTNUT, and PORK SOUP

SERVES 4

This is another moisturizing soup for the fall. Polygonatum and sand ginseng lubricate the body by conserving fluid in the organs, such as the skin and lungs. Water chestnuts relieve dryness and heat. Apricot kernels protect the lungs and remove phlegm.

1. Soak the polygonatum, sand ginseng, and apricot kernels in enough water to cover for 4 hours.

2. Wash and peel the water chestnuts. Split each piece in half.

3. Rinse the pork, and cut into small pieces. In a pot, blanch the pork in boiling water for 5 minutes, until the impurities rise to the surface. Discard the water and set the pork aside. Rinse out the pot.

4. Bring the 8 cups of water to a boil in the same pot. Add all of the ingredients, lower the heat to medium, and simmer for 1½ hours, until reduced to 4 cups.

5. Add salt to taste, 10 minutes before the soup is done. Strain and discard all the ingredients except the meat and water chestnuts, if desired.

2 ounces polygonatum
玉竹

1 ounce sand ginseng
沙參

1 ounce sweet apricot kernels 南杏

1/4 ounce bitter apricot kernels 北杏

6 water chestnuts

14 ounces lean pork

8 cups water

4 honey dates 蜜棗

Salt, for serving

TIPS

Use fresh water chestnuts, not canned ones. If you cannot find fresh water chestnuts, omit them from the recipe and use 3 or 4 frozen dried figs instead.

You can eat the meat and water chestnuts after you drink the soup.

PAPAYA, APRICOT KERNEL, AND SNOW FUNGUS SOUP

SERVES 4

2 pounds papaya

4 snow fungus 雪耳

1 ounce sweet apricot kernels 南杏

1/2 ounce bitter apricot kernels 北杏

14 ounces lean pork

8 cups water

Salt, for serving

This soup replaces and conserves moisture in the body and protects and strengthens the lungs against coughs due to dry weather. The key ingredient is papaya, which keeps the body moisturized. Snow fungus relieves coughs and dryness, improves yin energy, and nourishes the lungs. Apricot kernels (bitter and sweet) are excellent for the lungs, relieving shortness of breath, and they improve the appetite as well.

1. Rinse and peel the papaya, and discard the seeds. Cut into small pieces. Set aside.

2. Lightly rinse the snow fungus. Soak in enough water to cover for 30 minutes, or until softened. Separate each snow fungus into a few pieces; discard the core and water and set the fungus aside.

3. Lightly rinse the apricot kernels. Set aside.

4. Rinse the pork, and cut into small pieces. In a pot, blanch the pork in boiling water for 5 minutes, until the impurities rise to the surface. Discard the water and set the pork aside.

5. Rinse out the pot, and bring the 8 cups of water to a boil over high heat. Add all of the ingredients, including the reserved pork. Turn the heat down to medium, and cook for 2 hours, until reduced to 4 cups.

6. Add salt to taste, 10 minutes before the soup is ready. Discard the apricot kernels and enjoy.

TIPS

You can make this soup with Hawaiian or Mexican papayas, the most popular species available in North American markets.

This soup can also be made into a dessert. To do this, omit the meat and use rock sugar instead of salt.

Except for the apricot kernels, you can eat everything after you drink the soup.

❁

CHAPTER

9

WINTER

RECIPES

- Codonopsis, Chicken, and Fish Maw Soup

- Papaya, Chicken Feet, and Lily Bulb Soup

- Red Lingzhi with Chrysanthemum, Jujube, and Beef Soup

- Ox Shank Soup with Goji Berries, Jujube, and Longan

- Coconut, Polygonatum, and Conch Soup

- Chinese Yam, Goji Berry, and Black Chicken Soup

- Apricot Kernel Puree, Bok Choy, and Chicken Soup

- Ginseng with Rice Soup

- Codonopsis, Five-Finger Peach, Polygonatum, Chinese Yam, and Hyacinth Bean Soup

- Walnut, Astragalus Root, Chinese Yam, and Pork Shank Soup

inters vary from region to region. Some are wet and cold. Others are snowy, dry, and windy. During this time, it is necessary for the body to retain heat, expel coldness and dampness, and stay warm. If the cold and wind gets into your body, it can cause flu, the pores to close, and the blood vessels to contract. You will feel stuffy all over.

Winter is a good time to nourish and maintain your health. Properly conditioning your body in the winter will not only improve your immunity but also help you to cope with the season's many ups and downs. Most people eat more raw and cold foods during the summer and into the fall. The stomach suffers quite a lot when this happens.

Now, in the winter, it is necessary to warm our stomachs. In early winter, when the weather is slightly cold, eating mild food such as yams, chestnuts, and gorgon fruit can invigorate the spleen, stomach, and kidneys. In the deep winter, eating warmer energy foods like lamb and glutinous rice or drinking a small amount of alcohol will help to combat the cold.

It is important to maintain yang energy to keep out the cold. Herbs like ginseng and lingzhi mushrooms help with this, as do chrysanthemums, jujube, barley, and goji berries.

CODONOPSIS, CHICKEN, AND FISH MAW SOUP

SERVES 4

Fish maw is dried swim bladder, but don't let that discourage you from making this soup! It's considered quite a tasty delicacy in Cantonese cuisine, as it's known for its melt-in-your-mouth qualities. Fish maw nourishes the kidney, treats kidney deficiency, and strengthens muscles and veins. It makes an excellent tonic for postpartum women. Fish maw is also rich in high-grade collagen. If you regularly consume it, you will see that the food provides beauty and anti-aging effects.

1/2 aged chicken

3 ounces fish maw 魚肚

5 jujube 紅棗

1 ounce codonopsis 黨參

2 slices fresh ginger

8 cups water

Salt, for serving

1. Remove the head, neck, all the skin, and the fat from the chicken. Wash it and chop into small pieces.

2. Lightly rinse the fish maw. Soak in water to cover for 1 hour.

3. In a pot, boil the chicken and fish maw together for 5 minutes over high heat, until the impurities rise to the surface. Discard the water, set the meat aside, and rinse out the pot.

4. Lightly rinse the jujube and codonopsis. Soak together in enough water to cover for 30 minutes. Discard the water. Split the jujube in half and remove the pits. Chop the codonopsis into small pieces.

5. Place all of the ingredients in the pot. Add the 8 cups of water and bring to a boil over high heat. Lower the heat to medium-low, and cook for 2 hours.

6. Add salt to taste. Strain and discard all the ingredients except the chicken and fish maw, if desired.

TIPS

Aged chicken is just an older bird that you should be able to find at Chinese poultry shops. If you cannot find aged chicken, fresh chicken will do. If you are able to choose between purchasing a hen or a rooster, select the hen. According to Traditional Chinese Medicine, roosters (male chickens) are slightly toxic, as opposed to hens (female chickens), which are not.

The chicken will be sold whole, so discard the head and neck.

Fish maw is available in dried form at herbal stores. It varies in price from a few dollars per package to a few hundred dollars. Go with the inexpensive one for this recipe because the nutritional value is comparable between the two types.

You can eat the meat and fish maw after you drink the soup.

PAPAYA, CHICKEN FEET, AND LILY BULB SOUP

6 ounces chicken feet

10 ounces papaya

14 ounces pork shank

4 jujube 紅棗

2 ounces peanuts

2 ounces fresh lily bulb or 1 ounce dried 百合

1 tangerine peel 陳皮

4 honey dates 蜜棗

8 cups water

Salt, for serving

This healing soup has the power to calm nerves, invigorate the spleen, and moisturize the body during the harshest of winters. Chicken feet are rich in collagen and calcium. Over time, frequent consumption of them strengthens blood vessels and lowers blood lipids, blood pressure, and cholesterol. Chicken feet also beautify the skin, remove wrinkles, promote bone growth, and improve resistance to aging.

Jujube dates help to build up the blood supply. Lily bulb, honey dates, and papaya not only provide moisture for the body during winter, but each is extremely nutritious.

1. Lightly rinse the chicken feet.

2. Bring half a pot of water to a boil over high heat. Add the chicken feet for 5 minutes. Discard the water, and set aside the chicken feet.

3. Peel the papaya, remove the seeds, and cut the fruit into smaller pieces. Set aside.

4. Rinse the pork shank, remove the fat, and cut the meat into smaller pieces. In the same pot, blanch the pork in boiling water for 5 minutes, until the impurities rise to the surface. Discard the water and set the pork aside. Rinse out the pot.

5. Lightly rinse the jujube, peanuts, lily bulb, and tangerine peel. Remove and discard the pits from the dates.

6. Place all of the ingredients in the same pot with 8 cups of water. Bring to a boil over high heat, then turn the heat down to medium-low. Cook for 1½ hours, until the water is reduced to 4 cups.

7. Add salt to taste, 10 minutes before serving. Strain and discard the tangerine peel and honey dates.

TIPS

If you are allergic to peanuts, omit them from the soup.

Chicken feet can be bought in Chinese supermarkets.

You can eat the residue after you drink the soup.

RED LINGZHI WITH CHRYSANTHEMUM, JUJUBE, AND BEEF SOUP

SERVES 5

This soup is rich in nutrients and boosts immunity for the cold winter. Red lingzhi (commonly known as reishi mushrooms) are excellent at enhancing immunity. They allow the body to resist invading bacteria and viruses faster by strengthening the immune system. They also help to normalize high blood pressure and keep the liver healthy and strong. According to TCM, these mushrooms fight fatigue, depression, and cancer too! Chrysanthemum clears the body of heat. Both jujube and beef are good for blood production. Tangerine peel eliminates phlegm, dispels colds, relieves bloating, soothes the spleen, and helps with stomach qi stagnation.

1/4 ounce red lingzhi (dried) 赤靈芝

6 jujube 紅棗

11/2 ounces chrysanthemum flowers 菊花

14 ounces lean beef shank or stewing beef

1 tangerine peel 陳皮

10 cups water

Salt, for serving

1. Rinse the lingzhi and set aside.

2. Lightly rinse the jujube. Split each in half, discard the pits, and set the fruit aside.

3. Rinse the chrysanthemums and soak in enough water to cover for 10 minutes. Drain and set aside.

4. Rinse the beef and cut into small portions.

5. Lightly rinse the tangerine peel.

6. Place all the ingredients, except the lingzhi, in a pot with the 10 cups of water, and bring to a boil over high heat. Lower the heat to medium and cook for another 1½ hours.

7. Add the lingzhi 20 minutes before the soup is done. Cook until reduced to 5 cups.

8. Add salt to taste before serving. Strain and discard all the ingredients except the beef, if desired.

TIPS

We prefer to buy Hangzhou chrysanthemum flowers. They are grown in Zhejiang Province, China, and appear yellow in color.

You can eat the meat after you drink the soup.

OX SHANK SOUP WITH GOJI BERRIES, JUJUBE, AND LONGAN

SERVES 4

Winter is the best time to conserve energy. The ingredients in this recipe blend together to help our bodies build up qi reserves so that we can better protect ourselves against the season's coldness. Beef, a slightly hot food, aids the body in making energy. Goji berries contain iron and encourage blood production. Jujube also aids in blood production and improves qi. Longan is a sweet and smooth fruit that warms the body and benefits the heart and spleen. It replenishes qi and the blood supply, providing a nourishing and rejuvenating effect on the system.

14 ounces ox shank

1/2 ounce goji berries 枸杞

1 ounce dried longan 桂圓肉

6 jujube 紅棗

2 ounces Chinese yam (fresh or dried) 淮山

8 cups water

Salt, for serving

1. Clean and cut the ox shank into small pieces.

2. Rinse the goji berries and dried longan. Set aside.

3. Rinse the jujube, remove the pits, and set the fruit aside.

4. Rinse the Chinese yam, and soak in enough water to cover for 20 minutes.

5. Place all of the ingredients into a pot with the 8 cups of water. Bring to a boil over high heat, then reduce the heat to medium and simmer for 1½ hours, until reduced to 4 cups.

6. Add salt, as desired, before serving.

TIPS

Beef shank can be substituted for ox shank.

Black goji berries are superior to the red variety, but either works. When you are choosing among red goji berries, do not choose the bright red ones. Dyed counterfeit goji berries are rampant, so beware of merchants selling extremely bright red ones.

You can eat all the ingredients as you drink the soup.

COCONUT, POLYGONATUM, AND CONCH SOUP

SERVES 4

8 ounces fresh conch or 4 ounces dried 響螺

2 snow fungus 雪耳

6 ounces fresh coconut meat

1 ounce polygonatum 玉竹

4 jujube 紅棗

1/2 chicken

10 cups water

Salt, for serving

This warm and delicious tonic improves energy, conserves warmth, and is a mélange of flavors! Coconut is sweet and fragrant, while conch is salty and earthy without being too fishy. Conch improves yin energy and immunity. It also invigorates the spleen, stomach, and kidneys. Snow fungus invigorates the spleen, clears the intestines, strengthens the stomach, clears away heat, moisturizes, improves sleep, and replenishes qi.

1. If you are using frozen conch, wash it and soak it in water to cover for 2 to 3 hours, or until softened. When the conch has thawed, cut into small pieces and set aside. If you are using dried conch, wash it briefly and soak it in water for 2 hours. Discard the water. Add fresh water to the conch and soak overnight until softened. Use this water as part of the water for cooking the soup.

2. Lightly rinse the snow fungus. Then soak in enough water to cover for 1 to 2 hours, or until softened. Separate the flower body from the core and break into smaller pieces. Discard the core, and set the fungus aside.

3. Rinse the coconut meat and polygonatum and set aside.

4. Rinse the jujube and remove the pits. Set aside.

5. Rinse the chicken, remove the skin and fat, and cut the meat into small pieces.

6. Place all the ingredients with the 10 cups of water into a pot. Bring to a boil over high heat, then lower the heat to medium and simmer for 2 hours, until reduced to 4 cups.

7. Add salt, as desired, before serving. Discard the polygonatum before enjoying.

TIPS

You can leave the pits in the jujube when you cook them, but it makes the broth "hotter," which makes the soup less suitable for hot body types.

Avoid buying snow fungus that is extremely white in color, which could mean they are bleached. Bleached fungus is not as healthy.

You can eat all the ingredients with the soup except the polygonatum.

CHINESE YAM, GOJI BERRY, AND BLACK CHICKEN SOUP

SERVES 6

2 ounces Chinese yam (fresh or dried) 淮山

1/2 ounce goji berries 紅棗

1 (11/2- to 2-pound) black chicken (also known as a silkie)

10 cups water

Salt, for serving

Call this the chicken soup of Chinese culture. Black chickens are black from the inside out. Not only are their feathers and skin a dark color, but their bones, muscles, meat, and organs are also black. Black chicken is believed to be more nutritious than regular chicken. It is excellent for strengthening the body, getting rid of fatigue, and delaying aging. The bird nourishes yin and the kidneys and helps with iron deficiency and anemia in women. Black chicken contains more than nineteen kinds of amino acids, despite having low cholesterol and fat content. A great source of vitamin A, the meat also cleanses blood, regulates immune function, and heals menstrual disorders that are caused by a deficiency of qi.

Goji berries have similar benefits, in addition to potent anti-aging powers. They are a good source of iron and help to nourish the liver and improve eyesight. Chinese yam is good for the spleen and stomach.

1. Rinse the Chinese yam and goji berries. Soak the Chinese yam in enough water to cover for 20 minutes. Drain and set aside.

2. Rinse the black chicken. Discard any intestines and remove the skin. (Frozen chickens are usually already gutted.) Keep the bones. Cut the meat into small pieces. Blanch the chicken lightly in hot water for 5 to 10 minutes. Set aside. Discard the water.

3. Place the 10 cups of water and all of the ingredients in a pot. Bring to a boil over high heat. Then reduce the heat to medium and cook for 1½ hours, until reduced to 6 cups.

4. Add salt, as desired, before serving.

TIPS

Black chicken is sold in most Chinese supermarkets in the frozen foods section. There are two types of black chicken meat: one has nonblack feathers and black flesh, and the other type has black feathers and black flesh. The latter is more nutritious, but either type will work. If you cannot find black chicken, use regular chicken. If you purchase at a butcher shop, ask the butcher to gut the chicken for you. Do not use the chicken head or neck.

People with a cold or flu cannot drink this.

You can eat everything in the soup.

APRICOT KERNEL PUREE, BOK CHOY, AND CHICKEN SOUP

SERVES 5

8 ounces sweet apricot kernels 南杏

8 ounces bok choy

1/2 chicken

10 cups water

Salt, for serving

This is a warm, tasty, nutritious soup for the whole family, and it fits every type of body. Apricot kernels moisturize the lungs and relieve coughs and dryness of the throat against the coldness in winter. They also improve the production of body fluids and increase appetite. Bok choy is a delicious vegetable that is rich in nutrients, beta-carotene, vitamin B1, vitamin B2, vitamin C, crude fiber, protein, fat, calcium, phosphorus, and iron. It clears heat and lowers irritability, quenches thirst, protects against diuresis, and improves stomach health.

1. Lightly rinse the apricot kernels. Place in a blender with 1 cup of water and puree into a liquid. Set aside.

2. Rinse the bok choy and cut into small pieces. Set aside.

3. Rinse the chicken, and blanch in hot water for 5 minutes. When the impurities float to the top, turn off the heat and discard the water. Rinse the pot.

4. Place all the ingredients in the pot with the remaining 9 cups of water. Bring to a boil over high heat. Lower the heat to medium, and cook for another 1½ hours, until reduced to 5 cups.

5. Stir in salt, as desired, before serving.

TIPS

Soaking the apricot kernels for 30 minutes before putting them in the blender makes the kernels easier to work with.

Buy a hen rather than a rooster. Do not use the chicken head or neck.

You can eat the meat and bok choy with the soup.

❀ **Healing Herbal Soups**

GINSENG WITH RICE SOUP

SERVES 3

This is one of our lighter recipes of the season, and it happens to be vegetarian. Rice soup is rich in carbohydrates, vitamins B1 and B2, phosphorus, iron, inorganic salts, and other nutrients. It's sweet and invigorates qi, nourishes yin, and moisturizes. Rice soup is also good for strengthening the spleen and stomach. Cooked with ginseng, which is known for building up qi and blood production, this soup improves yin energy and strengthens the kidneys, spleen, and stomach. American ginseng, in particular, improves memory and enhances immunity. Because the herb is slightly on the cool side, we add ginger to the recipe to warm it up.

2 ounces Chinese yam (fresh or dried) 淮山

1 tangerine peel 陳皮

8 ounces white rice

1 ounce coix seeds 薏米

3 ounces American ginseng 花旗參

2 slices fresh ginger

6 cups water

Salt, for serving

1. Lightly rinse the Chinese yam. Then soak in water to cover for 20 minutes.

2. Soak the tangerine peel in water for 10 minutes, until softened.

3. Rinse the rice twice, with filtered water if possible, and set aside.

4. Lightly rinse all the other ingredients.

5. Place all of the ingredients and 6 cups of water in a pot. Cook over medium heat, stirring constantly to prevent the rice from becoming sticky.

6. When the soup begins to boil, turn the heat to low and simmer for 5 minutes. Do not cover with a lid. Then bring the soup back to a boil.

7. When the soup has reduced to 3 cups, it is ready.

8. Stir in salt as desired before serving. Strain and enjoy the broth.

TIPS

We prefer Texas long grain rice for this recipe. Do not use glutinous rice because it is too sticky. Instead of throwing the semicooked rice out, you can continue cooking it in a separate pot or rice cooker.

Stick to American ginseng because it is one of the milder varieties available.

Just drink the soup. Discard the other ingredients.

CODONOPSIS, FIVE-FINGER PEACH, POLYGONATUM, CHINESE YAM, AND HYACINTH BEAN SOUP

SERVES 4

3 ounces five-finger peach 五指毛桃

14 ounces lean pork

2 pieces codonopsis 黨參

1 ounce polygonatum 玉竹

2 ounces Chinese yam (fresh or dried) 淮山

2 ounces hyacinth bean 扁豆

8 cups water

Salt, for serving

This soup boosts immunity, strengthens chi, and dispels any dampness trapped in our bodies because of winter temperatures. Codonopsis is a bit like ginseng, but in a much milder form. The herb replenishes qi and nourishes blood by increasing the number of red blood cells and hemoglobin in the body. It also promotes the recovery of white blood cells, thereby ameliorating iron deficiency and anemia caused by malnutrition.

Five-finger peach improves immunity and helps to regulate blood pressure. Polygonatum is sweet, slightly cold, and beneficial for improving yin energy, and it is very moisturizing. The root strengthens the heart and lowers blood sugar. The methanol extract from polygonatum can significantly reduce some forms of hyperglycemia and moisturize skin too.

1. Lightly rinse all the ingredients.

2. Soak the five-finger peach in enough water to cover for 10 minutes. Discard the water.

3. Rinse the pork and cut into small pieces. In a pot, blanch the pork in boiling water for 5 minutes, until the impurities rise to the surface. Discard the water and set the pork aside. Rinse out the pot.

4. Put all the ingredients and the 8 cups of water in the pot. Bring to a boil over high heat, then lower the heat to medium and simmer for 1½ hours, until reduced to 4 cups.

5. Stir in salt to taste right before serving. Strain and discard all the ingredients except the meat, if desired.

TIPS

Try to buy organic five-finger peach. Several varieties are soaked with sulfur. Steer clear of these. One way to do this is to smell the five-finger peach before buying it. Natural ones have a sweet fragrance, while the sulfur-smoked ones smell funny.

You can eat the meat after you drink the soup.

WALNUT, ASTRAGALUS ROOT, CHINESE YAM, AND PORK SHANK SOUP

SERVES 4

This broth will make you smarter and healthier! Walnuts are good for the brain and kidneys. They are rich in protein, fatty acids, B vitamins, vitamin E, calcium, magnesium, and selenium. They can prevent cell aging, enhance memory, improve cholesterol absorption, moisturize the skin, and relieve fatigue and stress. Astragalus root is good for improving qi and circulation, while jujube is good for blood production. Chinese yam improves the health of the spleen and stomach and aids in the digestion of the soup overall.

2 ounces walnuts

1 ounce astragalus root 黃芪

6 jujube 紅棗

2 ounces Chinese yam (fresh or dried) 淮山

14 ounces lean pork

8 cups water

Salt, for serving

1. Rinse the walnuts and set aside.

2. Lightly rinse the astragalus root, jujube, and Chinese yam.

3. Split each jujube in half, and discard the pits.

4. Rinse the pork and cut into small pieces. In a pot, blanch the pork in boiling water for 5 minutes, until the impurities rise to the surface. Discard the water and set the pork aside. Rinse out the pot.

5. Place all the ingredients in the pot with the 8 cups of water. Bring to a boil over high heat, then lower the heat to medium and simmer for 1½ hours, until reduced to 4 cups.

6. Before serving, add salt to taste. Strain and discard all the ingredients except the meat and walnuts, if desired.

TIPS

If you have a cold or cough, make this soup without the astragalus root, which can worsen your condition.

You can eat the meat and walnuts after you drink the soup.

CHAPTER

10

IMMUNITY
SOUPS
and DRINKS

RECIPES

- Cordyceps Flower, Goji Berry, and Red Lingzhi Soup

- Three Bean Soup Drink

- Five-Finger Peach with Siberian Ginseng Soup

- Five-Finger Peach and Black Chicken Soup

- Seahorse, Sandworm, and Goji Berry Soup

- Drink for Poor Air Quality: Young Monk Fruit Water

- Drink to Relieve Stress: Flower Tea

s we write this book in 2021, the world is facing an unprecedented pandemic of the highly contagious respiratory illness known as COVID-19. Governments around the world have asked their citizens to stay home and refrain from conducting business outside—and especially not without masks on.

For health advocates like us, this global crisis illustrates how crucial it is to keep our immune system in tip-top shape. With that in mind, we have included this chapter of soups and beverages that you can drink throughout the year to retain your body's qi, the backbone of the immune system.

The best time to make and consume most of these superboosters is during the winter, and the least preferable time to drink them is during summer. Drink one weekly, or when you're feeling run down.

CORDYCEPS FLOWER, GOJI BERRY, AND RED LINGZHI SOUP

SERVES 4

Cordyceps flowers are not technically a flower; they are a cultured fruiting body that is a fungus. A neutral food that is high in fiber, they can enhance the immunity of the upper respiratory tract, relieve coughs, and prevent bronchitis. Lingzhi, better known as reishi mushrooms, are a warm food. They, too, can increase immunity against illnesses and are known for strengthening immune systems against cancer while strengthening the body. Goji berries are rich in iron, important for blood production and maintaining the health of the eyes and liver.

1 ounce cordyceps flowers 虫草花

1/2 ounce lingzhi 赤靈芝

1/2 ounce goji berries 枸杞

14 ounces lean pork

8 cups water

Salt, for serving

1. Gently rinse the cordyceps flowers. The spores on the flowers are essential. Unless the flowers are really dirty, be tender when rinsing because you do not want to wash the spores off.

2. Lightly rinse the lingzhi and goji berries. Set aside.

3. Rinse the pork and cut into small pieces. In a pot, blanch the pork in boiling water for 5 minutes, until the impurities rise to the surface. Discard the water and set the pork aside. Rinse out the pot.

4. Add the pork and lingzhi to the pot with the 8 cups of water. Bring to a boil over high heat. Then lower the heat to medium and cook for 1 hour, until reduced to 4½ cups.

5. Add the cordyceps flowers and cook for another 15 minutes, until the soup is reduced to 4 cups.

6. Add the goji berries to the soup and cook for another 15 minutes. Total cooking time should not exceed 2 hours.

7. Stir in salt to taste before serving. Strain and discard all the ingredients except the pork, if desired.

TIPS

Cordyceps flowers can be found at Chinese herbal pharmacies.

You can eat the pork after you drink the broth.

THREE BEAN SOUP DRINK

3 ounces adzuki beans
赤小豆

2 ounces mung beans
綠豆

3 ounces black beans
黑豆

2 ounces honeysuckle
金银花

1/2 ounce licorice root or rock sugar 甘草/冰糖

8 cups water

Three bean soup is perfect for the summer, especially on the hottest days. This sweet drink is an ancient formula that helps pregnant women with nausea and regulating blood pressure. The beverage also has other benefits, such as clearing pimples and strengthening the lungs. Black beans and licorice root detoxify as well as strengthen the kidneys and the spleen. Mung beans clear heat from the lungs, and adzuki beans dehumidify. The combination of these three ingredients leads to a general detoxification of the system. Once blockages are removed, the immune system performs better. Thus, the soup indirectly increases immunity against illnesses.

1. Soak all 3 beans in warm water for 1 hour. If you use licorice root instead of sugar, soak the licorice with the beans. Drain and discard the water.

2. Place the 8 cups of water in a pot and add all the beans and licorice, if using. Bring to a boil over high heat. Turn the heat down to medium and simmer for 1½ hours, until reduced to 4 cups.

3. Add the sugar, if using, 10 minutes before serving.

TIPS

People with gout, kidney stones, stomach issues, and infections cannot drink this soup as it may worsen their condition. Traditional Chinese Medicine does not recommend beans for these individuals.

You can eat the beans after you finish the drink.

Healing Herbal Soups

FIVE-FINGER PEACH WITH SIBERIAN GINSENG SOUP

SERVES 4

Siberian ginseng, which is widely used in Russia as an adaptogen, is a great immune system booster. It's not technically part of the ginseng family, but rather a woodsy shrub, and it has many uses. The plant relieves lung problems, improves bone strength, increases circulation, improves low blood pressure, accelerates the healing of wounds, strengthens memory, and boosts energy. Five-finger peach also invigorates energy and restores the immune system. Together with polygonatum, which moisturizes the lungs, builds yin, and rejuvenates the stomach, the tonic improves qi overall and revitalizes the immune system, especially against lung issues.

3 ounces five-finger peach 五指毛桃

1/4 ounce Siberian ginseng 刺五加

1 ounce polygonatum 玉竹

6 frozen figs 無花果

14 ounces lean pork

8 cups water

Salt, for serving

1. Lightly rinse the five-finger peach, ginseng, polygonatum, and figs and set aside.

2. Rinse the pork and cut into small pieces. In a pot, blanch the pork in boiling water for 5 minutes, until the impurities rise to the surface. Discard the water and set the pork aside. Rinse out the pot.

3. Place all of the ingredients and 8 cups of water in the pot and bring to boil over high heat. Then reduce the heat to medium and cook for 1½ hours, until reduced to 4 cups.

4. Add salt to taste, right before serving. Strain and discard all the ingredients except the pork, if desired.

TIPS

Individuals suffering from high blood pressure, diabetes, blood disorders, mental illness, heart problems, cancer, and heart issues cannot drink Siberian ginseng; it increases circulation and in turn promotes (both good and bad) cell growth and increases blood pressure. Pregnant women should also avoid Siberian ginseng.

People with high blood pressure can substitute ginseng with 1 ounce of codonopsis in the recipe.

You can eat the pork after drinking the soup.

FIVE-FINGER PEACH AND BLACK CHICKEN SOUP

SERVES 4

3 ounces five-finger peach 五指毛桃

1 ounce polygonatum 玉竹

1 ounce dried longan 桂圓肉

1 black chicken (also known as silkie)

8 cups water

Salt, for serving

Five-finger peach improves circulation and lessens blockages and pain while strengthening the spleen and dehumidifying the body all at once. Polygonatum restores the stomach and improves the secretion of body fluids. Longan pacifies nerves, supports blood supply, and restores the spleen. Black chicken is highly nutritious and revitalizes the blood supply, improves qi, and lifts the immune system so that it functions at a higher level.

1. Lightly rinse the peach, polygonatum, and longan and set aside.

2. For the black chicken, gut and clean thoroughly, and remove the skin. Cut the meat into small pieces.

3. Place all the ingredients in a pot with the 8 cups of water. Bring to a boil over high heat. Reduce the heat down to medium and cook for 2 hours, until reduced to 4 cups.

4. Add salt as desired before serving. Strain and enjoy the broth, discarding the other ingredients.

TIPS

A stew pot is preferred for cooking this soup. If you do use one, reduce the amount of water you use to 6 cups.

Black chicken is sold in most Chinese supermarkets in the frozen foods section. There are two types of black chicken meat: one has nonblack feathers and black flesh, and the other type has black feathers and black flesh. The latter is more nutritious, but either type will work. If you cannot find black chicken, use regular chicken. If you purchase at a butcher shop, always ask the butcher to gut the chicken. It will save you time. Do not use the chicken head or neck.

Drink just the broth.

SEAHORSE, SANDWORM, AND GOJI BERRY SOUP

SERVES 4

4 jujube 紅棗

14 ounces lean pork

1 pair of seahorses
(a male and a female)
海馬

1 ounce sandworms
沙蟲乾

1/2 ounce goji berries
枸杞

8 cups water

Salt, for serving

Chances are this recipe will change your views about marine life forever, and in a good way! Seahorses aren't just pretty to look at; they're actually a valuable (and expensive) item in TCM. They are known to revitalize the immune system, strengthen the heart, relax muscles, improve yang qi, and relieve coughs.

Sandworms are very potent and known as the ginseng of the sea in Chinese medicine. They are rich in protein and contain seventeen kinds of amino acids, as well as twelve kinds of trace elements, such as calcium, phosphorus, iron, zinc, manganese, magnesium, and cordycepin. Sandworms are known for their antibacterial, antiradiation, antiviral, antifatigue, anticancer, and anti-aging effects. They nourish yin, lower fire, clear lungs, and invigorate kidneys and yang qi. Sandworms strengthen the spleen and remove dryness as well.

Goji berries and jujube are all good for blood production since they contain iron and are also beneficial for the heart.

1. Lightly rinse all the dry ingredients.

2. Split the jujube in half and remove the pits.

3. Rinse the pork and cut into small pieces. In a pot, blanch the pork in boiling water for 5 minutes, until the impurities rise to the surface. Discard the water and set the pork aside. Rinse out the pot.

4. Place all the ingredients and the 8 cups of water in the pot. Bring to a boil over high heat. Lower the heat down to medium and simmer for 2 hours, until reduced to 4 cups.

5. Add salt before serving. Strain and discard all the ingredients except the jujube and pork, if desired.

TIPS

Sandworms cost $30 to $40 for 3 ounces. A male-and-female pair of seahorses costs $20 to $30. You can omit the sandworms from the recipe if they are out of your budget.

Pregnant women should not consume seahorse because it may affect the way reproductive hormones function.

We recommend using a stew pot. If you do, reduce the amount of water used to 6 cups.

You can eat the pork and jujube after you drink the broth.

DRINK FOR POOR AIR QUALITY:
YOUNG MONK FRUIT WATER

1 young monk fruit
羅漢果

8 cups water

Due to the extreme heat waves and forest fires that have become frequent, we are including this special drink to help those who live in these harmful, toxic environments. Young monk fruit water provides relief to the lungs and clears the toxins from any inhaled smoke.

This recipe was given to us by an amazing Chinese herbalist who formulated the drink years ago on a special assignment. He was working with a group of high-profile chain smokers who refused to give up their cigarettes but wanted something to protect them from emphysema and lung damage. The original intent of this simple beverage was to clear the toxins from tobacco use in the doctor's patients. After more than ten years of using this formula, our doctor friend said his patients who were consuming the drink frequently were still doing well, despite continuing to smoke.

This drink can help smokers but is not a cure-all for the ramifications caused by a harmful smoking habit.

1. Lightly rinse the monk fruit.

2. Using your hands, break the fruit up into pieces, including the shell and flesh.

3. Place the monk fruit and water in a pot, cover, and bring to a boil over high heat.

4. Turn the heat off but do not uncover the pot. Leave for 3 minutes.

5. Once the drink cools, it is ready to drink. You can keep it for up to 24 hours in the refrigerator.

TIPS

Young monk fruit is slightly yellow-green in color. Mature monk fruit is dark brown, which is not what you want. You may need to go to the counter of the herbal store (which assembles specialized decoctions) and ask for young monk fruit, as it is usually not available in the general merchandise area.

If you want to save time, you can break the monk fruit into 8 portions (with some skin and some flesh). Put a portion of it in a mug. Pour in boiling hot water. Cover the drink with a lid, let it brew for 5 minutes, and then drink the liquid.

Don't drink more than twice a day.

DRINK TO RELIEVE STRESS:
FLOWER TEA

SERVES 1

Whether it's mounting pressures at work or in the home, modern life is anything but relaxing. As a result, people are often stressed out and depressed. These feelings are not good for mental health, and they have a terrible effect on the liver. This popular tea combats these issues. It clears heat and detoxifies, soothes the liver, and regulates qi. Rosebuds relieve depression, reduce fire, and calm the mind and nerves. This drink is also good for colds, swelling, and sore throats.

There are many different versions of this type of flower tea. We are using a formulation that we think is the gentlest and safest.

2 teaspoons rosebud flowers 玫瑰

1 teaspoon chrysanthemum flowers 菊花

1/2 teaspoon jasmine flowers 茉莉花

1. Lightly rinse all of the ingredients and place in a mug. Pour boiling water into the mug, and cover for 5 to 7 minutes before drinking. Then sit back and relax.

TIPS

Keep in mind that the liver's resting time is from 1:00 a.m. to 3:00 a.m. That is why it is best to drink this tea in the evening because it gives you a good night's sleep.

Do not eat the flowers.

REFRESHING
SEASONAL DRINKS

Instead of cooking soups, which take time to make, here are recipes for a few healthy drinks for people who are on the go. Essentially these are quick teas. We don't include any for winter, because we encourage soups that need longer boiling time during winter months.

SPRING:
TANGERINE PEEL TEA

1/2 teaspoon tangerine peel 陳皮

1 teaspoon poria 茯苓

1 cup boiling water

Spring is full of dampness, which can hinder the effectiveness of the immune system. The spleen must be strengthened because it is the organ that removes dampness. This simple tea invigorates the spleen and helps reduce phlegm. Another benefit of the beverage is that it aids in weight loss because once the dampness is gone, your body can dissipate fat more easily.

1. Lightly rinse the tangerine peel and poria, and place in a mug.

2. Pour in the boiling water, and cover the mug for 5 minutes before drinking.

SUMMER: KOREAN MINT AND LOTUS LEAF TEA

SERVES 1

This is a fragrant tea that drives away summer heat and rids the body of dampness. Lotus leaf clears the heart of heat, relieves anxiety, and expels dampness. Bamboo leaves promote fluid and urine secretion, while lentil flowers invigorate the spleen. Korean mint is excellent at relieving heat and getting rid of dampness, as well as stopping diarrhea.

1. Lightly rinse the ingredients and place in a mug.
2. Pour in the boiling water, and cover the mug for 5 minutes before drinking.

1 teaspoon Korean mint 藿香

1 teaspoon lily leaf 荷葉

1 teaspoon lentil flower 扁豆花

1 teaspoon bamboo leaf 竹叶

1 cup boiling water

FALL: SNOW PEAR WATER

SERVES 1

Snow pear water helps to clear away heat and moisturize the body, break up phlegm, relieve coughs, remove dampness, detoxify, reduce swelling, and improve urination. Since snow pear has slightly cold properties, cooking it reduces the cold.

1. In a small saucepan, boil the coix seeds with the water until the seeds appear to split.
2. Remove the pit from the snow pear. Add the fruit to the saucepan and cook for 10 to 15 minutes before drinking.

1 ounce coix seeds (buy the slightly fried ones) 薏米(熟)

11/2 cups water

1/4 snow pear 雪梨

PART

III

OTHER USEFUL
INFORMATION

CHAPTER
11

DISPELLING MYTHS *about* GINGER, GINSENG, *and* TEA

GINGER

Ginger, a popular spice, is a hot type of food. Properly used, it can cure or prevent a lot of illnesses. According to Traditional Chinese Medicine, the plant is good for dispersing wind and cold trapped in the body, removing phlegm, and relieving coughs that are the result of cold weather (which usually happens in the spring and winter).

Once consumed, the herbaceous perennial heats up the body and can stop vomiting and nausea. Ginger warms the stomach and promotes detoxification. During hazy weather or when you feel carsick, you can chew (but not swallow) a few slices of ginger for a couple of minutes for instant relief.

But there are proper ways of eating ginger. Do not peel away the skin when you cook with it, never eat any ginger that has signs of rotting, and always consume in moderation—only once in a while and in small amounts.

BENEFITS OF GINGER

Ginger is especially helpful during the summer because it helps us sweat and feel refreshed afterward. Perspiration lowers our body temperature and relieves physical fatigue. When the weather is relatively hot, our body secretes less saliva and gastric juice. Because of this, we may feel less hungry than usual. Sometimes a few slices of ginger can help bring our appetite back.

Ginger water, which can be prepared at home like tea, can be a refreshing and helpful treat during the hot months. People who suffer heatstroke in the summer and drink a glass of ginger juice immediately often have instant relief.

You may notice that bacteria grow and multiply quickly during the summer, and as a result, food spoils easily. If you inadvertently consume food that has gone bad, eating some ginger helps with preventing and curing food-borne illness: ginger can kill oral and intestinal pathogens by acting like an antibiotic. That is why ginger water is sometimes used to treat morning breath and periodontitis.

When the weather is sweltering, people love to sit in front of an electric fan or an air-conditioner to enjoy the cold air. Unfortunately, this can subject you to colds easily, according to TCM. Once you feel you may be coming down with a cold, drink some ginger water. It will help expel cold from your body, preventing your condition from getting worse and helping you recover more quickly.

Year-round, ginger strengthens resistance to bacteria. It can effectively relieve stomach pain. Dried ginger powder relieves symptoms such as dizziness and vomiting, and the efficacy can last for more than four hours.

It is an old Chinese custom for women who have just given birth to drink ginger stew with pig feet and vinegar daily for a month. The belief is that drinking this special soup will help the mother dispel the cold she contracted during delivery, excrete toxins through menstrual flow, and nourish her with calcium from the soup to replenish the calcium she lost during pregnancy.

Some postpartum women go even further: they slice ginger (with the skin) and place it in hot water so that they can soak their feet for a few days after birth. It is quite effective for women looking to rejuvenate themselves. As a preventive measure, soaking your feet in ginger water eliminates certain problems that may pop up in a woman's later years, such as trembling hands and painful headaches.

SOAKING FEET WITH GINGER

Soaking feet with ginger has been practiced for centuries in China. As the pace of modern life increases, so does the amount of stress that our body endures, which in the long run can lead to a lot of small health issues. After a long day, soak your feet in hot water with ginger to get rid of fatigue and prevent disease. This will make you feel more relaxed and comfortable.

Soaking feet in ginger water helps to dissipate the cold and stimulate the acupuncture points of the feet. It is believed that all the organs of the body are connected to various points on the bottom of our feet. Ginger water improves blood circulation and qi, is helpful in unblocking the meridians, and speeds up metabolism. All this can strengthen your body overall and bolster your immune system.

To take full advantage of this requires learning how to properly soak our feet with ginger water and the precautions to take so that we do not cause damage to ourselves. Make sure you use old ginger (see page 180). Portion out half an ounce to an ounce (about half a medium-size piece of ginger) and flatten it with a kitchen knife. Boil in a covered saucepan with 5 cups of water for about 10 minutes, then pour into a basin or a bucket. Add an appropriate amount of cold water to adjust the water temperature to about 100°F. The water level should be below your ankles. Rub your feet while soaking them to speed up healing.

10 THINGS TO PAY ATTENTION TO WHILE SOAKING FEET

1. Do not soak your feet for more than 15 to 20 minutes. Make sure the water is not too hot or too cold. Use your hands to test the water, especially if you have problems sensing heat in your feet. As you soak your feet, blood will flow more to the lower limbs and less to the head.

2. Seniors, specifically those with cardiovascular and cerebrovascular diseases, need to make sure the water isn't too hot because it may induce hypertension and even stroke. They should stop soaking immediately if they feel tightness in their chest or dizziness.

3. People with high blood pressure or heart issues should avoid soaking their feet in ginger water.

4. Try not to use water that is too hot because it will destroy the sebum film on the skin's surface, causing dryness and itchiness.

has detoxing and disinfecting properties since it is a warm food. Seafood, especially shellfish, are extremely cold foods. Often a cold type of person will feel uncomfortable after eating cold food. Cooking shellfish with some ginger may help to prevent a bad situation.

GINGER SOUP

If you feel that grating ginger is too troublesome, you can make a soup with it instead. Continuous heating can fully release the effective ingredients in ginger, even if it is not freshly ground. The best choices for ginger soup are old or medium ginger.

1. Wash the ginger with the skin. Cut into 3 thin slices.
2. Place the ginger in a pot with 8 ounces of water.
3. Bring to a boil over high heat. Turn the heat to low heat and cook for 10 to 15 minutes and serve immediately.

When cooking ginger soup, you can add other ingredients according to your specific health needs or taste preferences. For example, when you need to quench your thirst in the summer, you can add sugarcane. When you need to expel coldness in your body during winter, you can add a tiny dash of pepper to the soup. To stop vomiting, add a dried dark plum (not preserved; you can buy them at Chinese supermarkets or herbal pharmacies). If you feel cold during your menstrual cycle, add a few dried jujube, which will help you to replenish energy, nourish your blood flow, improve your circulation, and make you feel better.

TOP 10 BENEFITS OF GINGER WATER

1. It prevents and treats colds.
2. For cold body types, it can reduce coldness in the hands and feet.
3. It promotes blood circulation and strengthens organs.
4. For women, it regulates menstruation and relieves symptoms such as dysmenorrhea.
5. It can effectively delay aging and prolong life.
6. It enhances metabolism, relieving fatigue and improving sleep quality.
7. It improves the dullness of the skin and brightens the complexion.
8. It drives away cold and air trapped in the body (which is believed to cause rheumatism). Soaking your feet can relieve symptoms of rheumatoid arthritis.
9. It stimulates sweat glands to discharge toxins.
10. It reduces or removes foot odor.

GINSENG

Ginseng is the national treasure, if not the superstar, of Traditional Chinese Medicine. There are different types of ginseng, and they differ tremendously in their effects. Overall, ginseng is a high-energy food that boosts the immune system and improves blood circulation, but eating the wrong type of ginseng can do more harm than good.

TYPES OF GINSENG

Ginseng is divided into five main categories: white ginseng, red ginseng, American ginseng, fresh ginseng, and wild ginseng.

WHITE GINSENG

This is a low-grade ginseng selected from inferior Korean ginseng, then boiled in water and dried in the sun. It comes packaged as small slices at herbal stores and is occasionally available ground into powder. Harvested after five years, the color of the surface of white ginseng is white or light yellow-white. When picking out white ginseng, choose one with a big branch that has old skin and long roots. White ginseng replenishes vitality, nourishes the mind, calms nerves, and prolongs life. There are many ways to take it. It can be used to make wine and soup, or it can be used as medicine.

RED GINSENG

Most commonly grown in Korea, red ginseng is steamed first, then dried. This process turns the ginseng red, hence its name. It usually comes packaged as small slices at herbal stores and is seldom ground into powder. Red ginseng has a translucent texture and is suitable for people with weak qi and a yang deficiency. It replenishes vitality and strengthens the spleen and stomach.

AMERICAN GINSENG

American ginseng, produced in Canada and the United States, is consumed in stews, lozenges, or as a ground powder. This species nourishes yin and the kidneys, replenishes vitality, nourishes the heart, and soothes the nerves. It can also lower body temperature. One of its special features is that it is invigorating without causing excess fire-heat, which some types of ginseng are prone to do.

FRESH GINSENG

Fresh ginseng is farmed under controlled conditions, and thus retains the advantages of many different kinds of ginseng. It is usually harvested a few months after planting. This species is quite mild and can be consumed, more often than other types of ginseng, mostly in soups. You can find it in the frozen foods section of some Asian supermarkets, especially Korean ones.

WILD GINSENG

With urbanization, wild ginseng is extremely hard to find and usually quite expensive for that reason. The most famous wild ginseng is found in the Changbai Mountains in Northeast China. It grows hidden in deep forests and on cliff areas. Wild ginseng is of high medicinal quality. In ancient Chinese folklore, there are mystical stories about what it takes to capture top-grade, really old wild ginseng. It is believed that this type of ginseng can "move" from place to place. And since it is so old, its skin has a bright, glistening layer that can be seen only under moonlight. That is why in all the tales, hunters start their search for ginseng late at night, shining torches through the forests to see if they can find the elusive plant. When they identify it, they shoot an arrow into it to stop it from moving. When daylight comes, they locate the arrow and the ginseng.

While the legend of wild ginseng is rooted in hearsay, the one true—but peculiar—fact about it is that wherever it grows, the land will be infertile for years with no other vegetation around it. The Chinese believe that is because the plant has drawn all the energy from the earth. It takes years for the land to gather back its nutrients and strength for other plants to grow.

Suffice it to say, wild ginseng is powerful stuff! And the older the ginseng is, the higher the medicinal value is. Old wild ginseng (say, twenty years old) goes for thousands of dollars on the market. While most people do not need this expensive ginseng unless they are seriously ill, wild ginseng is a powerful qi builder and has the ability to rejuvenate general functions of the body because it contains a lot of energy. Qi brings better circulation into the system, which benefits all organs. With more oxygen and nutrients, metabolism improves. It is believed that wild ginseng also delays the aging process if eaten moderately (a few months out of a year) and over the long term.

SUGAR GINSENG

This type of ginseng is made by soaking fresh ginseng in sugar water and then piercing several small holes in the plant with a needle. After soaking in the liquid, the plant is taken out to dry. Sugar ginseng is gentle and known for nourishing the body and moisturizing the lungs.

SUN-DRIED GINSENG

Most ginseng farmers turn their fresh ginseng into dried ginseng. Farm-grown ginseng is less effective than the kind grown in the wild. Dried ginseng replenishes qi and blood. It can also improve immunity and disease resistance when taken in moderation. It is usually sold packaged in boxes at Chinese supermarkets and herbal pharmacies, with a few naturally dried ginseng in each box.

No matter what kind of ginseng you buy, the way to distinguish its age is through the "stem" above the top part of the ginseng. Each stratum on the stem represents approximately a year's growth. Thus, the more strata the stem has, the older it is. Always examine the ginseng to see if it's worth the price being charged.

DOS AND DON'TS OF GINSENG

A ginseng dosage must be strictly controlled, taken in small amounts and in moderation.

Ginseng has hot and cold types too:

HOT GINSENG: White ginseng, red ginseng

WARM GINSENG: Fresh ginseng

COLD GINSENG: American ginseng, white ginseng

NEUTRAL GINSENG: Wild ginseng

Be aware of your body type before you take it. For example, hot body types should not take hot types of ginseng, and cold types of bodies should not take cold ginseng because it will cause blood pressure to lower, and you may experience dizziness or other symptoms like feeling weak.

White ginseng increases circulation and body temperature. It can also increase blood pressure beyond normal, so people with high blood pressure should avoid taking this type of ginseng. It can also cause dreams and insomnia by overstimulating the brain.

You should never take ginseng when you have a flu or cold or heatstroke. It will worsen your condition rapidly.

When you eat ginseng is important. Generally, autumn and winter are the most suitable for taking ginseng, and summer is not recommended. Also be aware of the time of the day you take it. It should be taken only during the day, not in the evening because it overstimulates the nervous system. Ginseng can affect sleep if it is taken too late at night.

Traditional Chinese Medicine believes that ginseng should not be taken with Chinese medicines such as acacia locustor or with foods rich in tannins, such as grapes, pomegranates, and tea. These foods will affect the effectiveness of ginseng.

After taking ginseng, do not eat turnips or drink soup with turnips because the vegetable will neutralize all the effects of ginseng. Conversely, if you eat the wrong ginseng and don't feel well, drinking turnip soup can relieve you.

Cooking ginseng has restrictions. Use porcelain pots or earthenware, not metal containers or pots because the chemical content of ginseng will not brought out properly and may clash with the properties of metal cookware.

has detoxing and disinfecting properties since it is a warm food. Seafood, especially shellfish, are extremely cold foods. Often a cold type of person will feel uncomfortable after eating cold food. Cooking shellfish with some ginger may help to prevent a bad situation.

GINGER SOUP

If you feel that grating ginger is too troublesome, you can make a soup with it instead. Continuous heating can fully release the effective ingredients in ginger, even if it is not freshly ground. The best choices for ginger soup are old or medium ginger.

1. Wash the ginger with the skin. Cut into 3 thin slices.
2. Place the ginger in a pot with 8 ounces of water.
3. Bring to a boil over high heat. Turn the heat to low heat and cook for 10 to 15 minutes and serve immediately.

When cooking ginger soup, you can add other ingredients according to your specific health needs or taste preferences. For example, when you need to quench your thirst in the summer, you can add sugarcane. When you need to expel coldness in your body during winter, you can add a tiny dash of pepper to the soup. To stop vomiting, add a dried dark plum (not preserved; you can buy them at Chinese supermarkets or herbal pharmacies). If you feel cold during your menstrual cycle, add a few dried jujube, which will help you to replenish energy, nourish your blood flow, improve your circulation, and make you feel better.

TOP 10 BENEFITS OF GINGER WATER

1. It prevents and treats colds.
2. For cold body types, it can reduce coldness in the hands and feet.
3. It promotes blood circulation and strengthens organs.
4. For women, it regulates menstruation and relieves symptoms such as dysmenorrhea.
5. It can effectively delay aging and prolong life.
6. It enhances metabolism, relieving fatigue and improving sleep quality.
7. It improves the dullness of the skin and brightens the complexion.
8. It drives away cold and air trapped in the body (which is believed to cause rheumatism). Soaking your feet can relieve symptoms of rheumatoid arthritis.
9. It stimulates sweat glands to discharge toxins.
10. It reduces or removes foot odor.

GINSENG

Ginseng is the national treasure, if not the superstar, of Traditional Chinese Medicine. There are different types of ginseng, and they differ tremendously in their effects. Overall, ginseng is a high-energy food that boosts the immune system and improves blood circulation, but eating the wrong type of ginseng can do more harm than good.

TYPES OF GINSENG

Ginseng is divided into five main categories: white ginseng, red ginseng, American ginseng, fresh ginseng, and wild ginseng.

WHITE GINSENG

This is a low-grade ginseng selected from inferior Korean ginseng, then boiled in water and dried in the sun. It comes packaged as small slices at herbal stores and is occasionally available ground into powder. Harvested after five years, the color of the surface of white ginseng is white or light yellow-white. When picking out white ginseng, choose one with a big branch that has old skin and long roots. White ginseng replenishes vitality, nourishes the mind, calms nerves, and prolongs life. There are many ways to take it. It can be used to make wine and soup, or it can be used as medicine.

RED GINSENG

Most commonly grown in Korea, red ginseng is steamed first, then dried. This process turns the ginseng red, hence its name. It usually comes packaged as small slices at herbal stores and is seldom ground into powder. Red ginseng has a translucent texture and is suitable for people with weak qi and a yang deficiency. It replenishes vitality and strengthens the spleen and stomach.

AMERICAN GINSENG

American ginseng, produced in Canada and the United States, is consumed in stews, lozenges, or as a ground powder. This species nourishes yin and the kidneys, replenishes vitality, nourishes the heart, and soothes the nerves. It can also lower body temperature. One of its special features is that it is invigorating without causing excess fire-heat, which some types of ginseng are prone to do.

FRESH GINSENG

Fresh ginseng is farmed under controlled conditions, and thus retains the advantages of many different kinds of ginseng. It is usually harvested a few months after planting. This species is quite mild and can be consumed, more often than other types of ginseng, mostly in soups. You can find it in the frozen foods section of some Asian supermarkets, especially Korean ones.

Pregnant women can take ginseng only under guidance of a licensed herbalist. People with cancer must avoid it because it increases cell growth, including cancer cell growth, with devastating effects.

TEA

There are many varieties of tea, and not all are good for your body type, so think before you drink! Here we discuss four main types of tea—red tea, black tea, green tea, and white tea—and focus on the ones that are mainly served within Chinese cuisine.

All teas do not all belong to the same food types, and they affect us differently. Because of different processing methods, the end product of tea becomes either hot, warm, cold, or neutral. Those with cold body types should drink warm tea; people with hot body types should drink cold tea.

Because of our complicated urban lifestyles, it is hard to distinguish between absolute cold types of bodies and absolute hot types of bodies. Many of us have mixed body types. For example, a heavy person can be very irritable (a symptom of a hot type of body), and yet if they eat a little cold food, they may get diarrhea easily, putting them into the cold body type category. Another person can be thin, with a weak spleen and stomach (cold body type characteristics), but belong to a hot body type category. In order to choose the right tea, base your assessment on your symptoms. You know your health best, so go with your intuition and observations.

The fermentation and processing of tea results in different teas becoming hot, cold, warm, or neutral foods. When the tea leaves go through fermentation, tea polyphenols are converted into theaflavins, thearubigins, and thearfuscins. As the color of the tea leaves deepens, the tea's properties become milder.

Following are the more common types of tea categorized into food types (note that generally, the more fermented a tea, the warmer its food properties):

HOT TEA: Black teas, such as Qimen tea (祁門紅茶), are fully fermented teas that don't irritate the stomach. Dark teas, such as ripe Pu'erh tea (普洱茶) and Liu Bao tea (六堡茶), are fully fermented teas.

WARM TEA: Dahongpao (大紅袍) has a higher degree of fermentation than Tieguanyin (鐵觀音). Both go through a carbon roasting process.

NEUTRAL TEA: Oolong tea (烏龍茶) has a moderate degree of fermentation. A popular oolong tea is Iron Goddess tea (also known as Tieguanyin).

COLD TEA: Green tea, white tea, and yellow tea (黃茶) are classified as cold teas due to their relatively low degree of fermentation.

Pay attention to the weather before you choose a tea. Oolong is good for autumn, while warm or hot teas like Pu'erh tea and black tea help warm the stomach in winter. In the spring, we should try to drink flower teas, such as chrysanthemum and rose tea, because they clear the dampness in our bodies. Colder teas should be consumed in the summer months; green tea is suitable for helping us get rid of heat.

Green tea is refreshing and helps to relieve thirst too. It also helps to clear the lungs of those who smoke tobacco or consume a lot of alcohol. One TCM study found that drinking hot green tea in the summer for nine minutes dropped the participants' average skin temperature by 1 to 2 degrees Celsius. Instead of drinking iced drinks, consume hot green tea to feel cooler.

Women who are menstruating should avoid drinking green tea because it may increase their flow due to the tea's cold nature. Once their menstrual period is over, they should drink teas that will help iron absorption, such as Old Metal Guanyin tea, ginger tea, rose tea, and goji berry tea.

People with allergies are prone to vomit when they drink green tea. Since there is no fermentation in the production process, the nutrient and chlorophyll contents are higher than other types of tea. Therefore, it can be more irritating to the stomach and intestines. People with ulcer or stomach issues should not drink green tea. Drinking young Tieguanyin (Iron Goddess) tea on an empty stomach causes discomfort because it is only slightly fermented.

When we eat a lot of deep-fried foods or stay up late, we may feel the "fire" or heat rising in our bodies. To "drop the fire," drink chrysanthemum tea, honeysuckle tea, mint tea, or rose tea.

Following are lengthier descriptions of special teas that we have mentioned and some others that you may have heard of. All of these teas help to "drop the fire" and make you feel relaxed and cool.

TIEGUANYIN (IRON GODDESS) TEA

During the fermenting and processing period, the tea leaves are roasted, cooled and sealed, and then stored in a special warehouse for ripening. Tieguanyin is divided into five grades, depending on how long it has been stored. Aim for teas that have been stored from ten to twenty-eight years. Tieguanyin Old Tea is recognized as the best tea among all the Tieguanyin teas.

Tieguanyin tea is a good drink for preventing heatstroke and to promote cooling. During extremely hot summers, a cup of hot or cold Tieguanyin tea will make you feel refreshed and cool, physically and mentally. It drives away the heat and replenishes fluids in your body.

CHRYSANTHEMUM TEA

A popular drink in Chinese households, chrysanthemum tea is known to clear heat and remove "fire." It can also help to clear dampness and heat in the eyes and clean toxins from the liver, thus improving the overall health of the eyes and eyesight. When Rose was young, she, like many other children in Asia, frequently developed small sties on her eyelids. To combat this, her mother boiled chrysanthemums and placed them on Rose's eyelids. The treatment was highly effective, and the sties went away very quickly.

To make tea for one serving, put ½ ounce of chrysanthemum, 3 to 4 dried goji berries, and 1 cup water in a pot, and slowly simmer for 10 minutes. It's best for people who feel hot and dry or suffer from lack of sleep.

HONEYSUCKLE TEA

A great tea for dispelling heat and dispersing "fire," honeysuckle tea is sweet in taste and has cold properties. It can effectively relieve minor inflammation and encourages detoxification. It is also used as medicine. In TCM studies, the plant was shown to resist pathogenic microorganisms and have a certain inhibitory effect on a variety of pathogenic bacteria. But beware: honeysuckle is a slightly cold food, so it is not suitable for women with cold bodies. Women who are menstruating should not drink this tea.

LILY TEA

Golden in color, sweet and slightly bitter in taste, lily tea is mainly produced in China and Japan. It can relieve heat and reduce "fire" and cool and moisturize the lungs. Lily is rich in various trace elements such as protein, sugar, phosphorus, and iron and has high medicinal and nutritional value.

THREE FLOWER TEA

This tea is made by mixing three kinds of flowers: Hangbai chrysanthemum (grown in Hangzhou), wild chrysanthemum, and honeysuckle; they are available in most Chinese supermarkets. A popular Chinese household drink, especially during summer, this flower tea is suitable for everyone to drink. (See Chapter 10 for our recipe.) This combination clears heat and detoxifies, calming the liver and improving eyesight. You can also add a little bit of honey, which also helps to clear heat.

TANGERINE TEA

This is one of our favorite teas. For one serving, lightly rinse ½ ounce of dried tangerine peel, tear it into small pieces, and place it in a teacup. Pour in boiling water, cover the cup with a lid, and let it steep for about 10 minutes. Add a small amount of honey. Chill in the refrigerator if you want to drink it cold. Tangerine tea is ideal for summer because it helps to relieve heat and coughs, removes phlegm, and invigorates the stomach.

LOTUS SEED HEART TEA

This is known to detox the body and protect the heart. To make the perfect mug, boil I cup of water with ½ ounce of lotus seed hearts. Then reduce the heat and simmer for 5 to 10 minutes. Lotus seed hearts can dispel heat, pacify the mind, and cure thirst and red eyes that result from too much heat.

EYE TEA

This is a tea for improving the eyes. Since we work with computers and cell phones daily, our eyes have become exhausted and stressed. A tea made with I ounce each of dried goji berries, white chrysanthemum, and raw, sun-dried fresh ginseng can effectively relieve eye fatigue, reduce stress, and calm the mind.

Drinking the right type of tea improves your health. It also helps to discipline your mind and body to exist in a more tranquil state. A cup a day is sure to keep your worries at bay!

12

DOS *and* DON'TS *of* TRADITIONAL CHINESE MEDICINE

I n Chapter 1, we explained what Traditional Chinese Medicine is and what its major components are. Then we explained how to incorporate medicinal eating into your life through making Chinese herbal soups and drinks. If you are now at a point where you are seriously contemplating exploring TCM more fully, we have some advice for you.

DOS *and* DON'TS *of* FINDING *a* PRACTITIONER

To locate a TCM practitioner, make sure you find one who is certified in both acupuncture and Chinese herbology. (Not everyone is.) Sometimes you will need to be administered herbs and acupuncture together, so why go to two specialists when you can go to one?

Ask your friends and family for recommendations. The best practitioners attended medical university in Asia and obtained a doctorate. In China, an herbalist is allowed to practice only after completing medical school and a vigorous residency, which involves rotations in different fields of medicine. This means they spend about ten years in higher education, much like physicians in the Western world do.

In the United States, less schooling is required for certified practitioners of Traditional Chinese Medicine. The rules depend on what state a practitioner wants to get licensed in and what his or her specialty is (acupuncture, Chinese herbology, Asian bodywork therapy, or Oriental medicine). A majority of states require practitioners to pass the National Certification Commission for Acupuncture and Oriental Medicine examination. You can go to the commission's website to search for a qualified Chinese herbalist and acupuncturist.

DOS *and* DON'TS *of* ACUPUNCTURE

Acupuncture is a clinical science in which very thin needles are inserted through the skin at strategic points on the body. The practice is used to stimulate the meridian system (meridian points) of the human body under the guidance of TCM theory, thereby preventing and curing disease.

A large number of recent clinical studies have shown that acupuncture has a multitude of uses. It stimulates the body's meridian system to play a regulatory role, affects various systems of the body, increases production of appropriate neurotransmitters and hormones, changes physiological functions, and achieves the purpose of curing diseases. For example, acupuncture can stimulate the function of a patient's adrenal glands to help secrete hormones, essentially achieving the same therapeutic effect as steroids but avoiding the side effects of Western drugs.

Acupuncture cannot treat cancer, but it can improve the quality of life in patients and help them complete chemotherapy and electrotherapy in accordance with their schedule, so that they can recover more quickly. Often people combine acupuncture with Western medicine. The therapeutic effect of acupuncture depends on the personal experience of the acupuncturist.

Acupuncture is an important practice in TCM and can be used alone to treat diseases. However, it can only improve, not cure, a patient's symptoms with some diseases, such as Parkinson's disease, brain degeneration, diabetes, and high blood pressure. Acupuncture treatment is highly effective on pain, gynecological diseases, insomnia, and gastrointestinal discomfort. Of course, the effect of taking Chinese medicine while undergoing acupuncture is ideal. The use of acupuncture to treat a disease is a process, and it depends on the condition and how long a person has had it. Like physical therapy, it takes time to get better.

According to TCM, humans have meridians circulating around the body that can be detected only in a living human being. (They cannot be detected in a corpse because it is an energy flow that ceases once the body dies.) It is believed that these meridians allow the qi to run and help the blood to circulate better. If qi is blocked, it will cause pain and other issues in the area of blockage, which will cause that portion of the body to malfunction.

Because pain is caused by a blockage, acupuncture is most effective for pain and nervous system–related illnesses as it helps to unblock and allow the qi to flow naturally again so that normal functions can resume.

Acupuncture works with most illnesses, but in order to make it work well, the patient needs to do it daily, which is impractical and expensive. That is why we need herbal decoctions or culinary medicine like drinking soups to sustain us between visits.

On top of that, certain illnesses are caused by a lack of yin or yang substances that can be improved only by consuming certain foods. This is another place where herbal soups and herbal decoctions come in. Mere stimulation by acupuncture will not work.

When you go into an acupuncture appointment, there are a few things to avoid. Do not receive acupuncture on an empty stomach. But don't eat a heavy meal before or after the session either. Refrain from drinking caffeinated or alcoholic beverages before and after the treatment because you cannot have substances that affect the activity of the nervous system. Please do not brush your tongue so that your practitioner can examine it correctly. Finally, remember to drink plenty of water after your treatment.

ROSE'S STORY

I had a terrible acupuncture experience once. I had had bad hay fever for weeks and was sneezing a lot and felt itchy all over. There seemed to be no end in sight. Seeing how badly I was doing, two of my acquaintances referred me to an acupuncturist.

I went to this acupuncturist to feel better. Secretly, however, I wanted to avoid my regular Chinese herbalist because I was tired of drinking the bitter decoctions he was giving me. My herbalist was very old school. He said if I drank his herbs twice a day, my allergies would go away in a week. I didn't want to go through the hard work of boiling herbs and drinking them. I wanted a shortcut to relief.

After the visit to this new acupuncturist, I immediately regretted my decision. Although I stopped sneezing, I began to feel very weak, lost my appetite, felt awful all night, and could not sleep. The next morning, I quickly went to see my herbalist, whom I had avoided—foolishly, as it turned out.

My herbalist discovered that the acupuncturist had blocked all the points where my nose secretions normally came through. Several points around my sinus areas were blocked, which affected the way my qi circulated. Because my whole energy flow had been disrupted, I felt awful. My herbalist actually said my qi was flowing in the opposite direction!

My herbalist helped me unblock the points immediately through acupuncture, and I felt better. He then asked that I drink another round of bitter herbs for a week to ensure that my energy flow returned to normal.

I am sharing this story because I want to stress that true healing does not take place overnight. If a practitioner tells you that you can be cured with one visit, something is wrong. I am also telling this story to reiterate that it is important to go to a doctor who knows how to prescribe herbs *and* perform acupuncture. You never know which one you'll need more, or whether you'll need both.

DOS *and* DON'TS *of* CUPPING

While acupuncture is the most popular TCM therapy around the world, cupping is probably one of the trendier ones in the West.

During a cupping session, a practitioner places round cups directly on a patient's skin— usually the back. The cup is either first heated with fire or manually pumped to create a suction. The cups are then left on the patient's skin for several minutes. During this time, the patient may feel the sensation of their skin rising inside the cups. At a certain point, the cups are removed. Round circular bruises are likely to remain.

According to TCM, the marks contain harmful and toxic substances that have been brought to the skin's surface. Once these marks fade, it's a sign that the toxins are no longer in a person's body. Cupping is widely used for pain relief and musculoskeletal injuries, such as strains, sprains, back injuries, and inflammation.

A more detailed explanation is that cupping takes the cold qi out of our bodies. This is why cupping is beneficial when we suffer from certain illnesses caused by cold energy trapped inside, such as a winter cold.

It's important to know that at the same time, the process of cupping also leaks out our good qi. That is why it is recommended that cupping not be exercised for more than five minutes. Too much cupping will harm you more than help you, because if you lose too much good qi, your immune system will weaken. Then the exterior cold and dampness will move into your body more easily, causing rheumatism or similar issues.

Cupping must be applied with caution and by TCM professionals. It is not uncommon to hear hair-raising stories about people who had too much cupping done and lost strength all over their body that took months of drinking herbal medicines to restore! (A little-known fact is that it is actually easier to restore acupuncture gone wrong than cupping gone wrong.)

Here are behaviors to follow should you want to maximize the benefits of your cupping session:

FOR 4 TO 6 HOURS AFTER CUPPING, AVOID EXPOSURE TO:

1. Caffeine, alcohol, sugary foods and drinks, dairy, and processed meats, which slow your body's ability to process the treatment
2. Hot showers, saunas, hot tubs, and strong air-conditioning
3. Intense exercise
4. Cold and windy conditions

AFTER YOUR VISIT

1. Immediately drink water or eat a spoonful of honey or some dates.
2. Rest for 10 to 15 minutes before exerting yourself.
3. Rub black seed oil, olive oil, or another natural oil over the cupped areas.
4. Eat fresh fruits and vegetables, or drink fresh juice.
5. Reduce dairy products for 24 hours.
6. Drink lots of water.
7. Avoid large meals and greasy foods.
8. Don't shower immediately after cupping.
9. Keep the areas that were treated covered and warm.
10. You may feel fatigued or experience flu-like symptoms the next day.

❁

CHAPTER
13

Q&A *with*

DR. SHIU
HON CHUI

Because we are home chefs and not medical professionals, we felt it was necessary to sit down with somebody who was more qualified to elaborate on concepts we discuss in this book. We turned to Dr. Shiu Hon Chui, a respected TCM practitioner, researcher, and professor friend of ours who lives in Hong Kong.

WHAT ARE YOUR ACADEMIC AND PROFESSIONAL QUALIFICATIONS?

Academic Qualifications

PhD in Chinese medicine, Hong Kong Baptist University (2004)

PhD in clinical biochemistry, Chinese University of Hong Kong (1990)

Professional Qualifications

Fellow of the Institute of Biomedical Sciences, United Kingdom (since 1977)

Fellow of the Royal Society of Chemistry, United Kingdom (since 1991)

Chartered Scientist, Royal Society of Chemistry, United Kingdom (since 2006)

Registered Part I Medical, Laboratory Technologist, Medical Laboratory Technologists Board, Hong Kong (since 1991)

Accredited Clinical Biochemist, Hong Kong Society of Clinical Chemistry (since 1994)

Registered Chinese Medicine Practitioner, Chinese Medicine Council of Hong Kong (since 2003)

WHAT HAVE YOU ACCOMPLISHED?

I am the chief executive officer of Diagnostix Group. I was a principal lecturer at the Department of Health Sciences of the former Hong Kong Polytechnic from 1978 to 1991. I then established a clinical laboratory, the Diagnostix Group, which was the first private laboratory accredited by the National Association of Testing Authorities (NATA) and Royal College of Pathologists of Australasia in Australia. In 2001, I set up an accredited Chinese medicine clinic, Modern TCM Limited. In 2005, I was invited to establish the first NATA-accredited clinical laboratory in Macau. I was also an associate professor at the Faculty of Health Sciences at Macau University of Science and Technology, and the deputy director of Macau Institute for Applied Research in Medicine and Health. From 2015 to 2019, I was appointed an honorary member of the Oncology Group of Chinese Medicine Expert Committee, the Association of Medical and Health Exchanges across the Taiwan Strait.

I have published fourteen books on Chinese medicine. I am also an academic adviser to several traditional Chinese medicine magazines and websites and I continue to publish clinical research papers in international medical journals.

WHEN PEOPLE ASK YOU WHAT TRADITIONAL CHINESE MEDICINE IS, WHAT DO YOU TELL THEM?

Traditional Chinese Medicine (TCM) is an important component of Chinese culture, which has developed for more than three thousand years. It is the accumulation of the experience of the Chinese in the effort to maintain health and treat diseases.

The science of TCM is the study of human pathophysiology, diagnosis, prevention, and treatment of disease. It is a theoretical system based on clinical experience and is mainly guided by a holistic concept based on the theories of yin-yang, five elements, viscera, and meridians. Treatment is planned according to syndrome diagnosis.

WHY IS IT IMPORTANT TO DRINK CHINESE HERBAL SOUPS?

Chinese people like boiling soup (especially southerners, including people in Hong Kong). When they are not sick, the soup can be used for body conditioning and disease prevention. It can also be used for initial treatment or alleviation of illness at the beginning of an illness. This combination of food ingredients with medicinal herbs is the proof of TCM's use of diet as medicine. According to the climate and your personal physique, the use of soup to achieve different purposes, such as clearing away heat, dehumidifying, and moisturizing, is usually suitable for young and old and can produce general or targeted conditioning effects. Over time, the yin and yang of the body are properly adjusted to balance easily, and the qi and blood are at healthy levels. There is a Chinese saying, "When the righteous qi is restored in the body, evil cannot interfere." When this happens, the body's disease resistance is often high, the chance of disease is reduced, and aging may be delayed.

DO ALL CHINESE DRINK SOUP DAILY?

Not all Chinese people like to drink soup, especially northerners, who do not place as much emphasis on soup. But southerners—such as those who live in Guangzhou and Hong Kong—are more accustomed to drinking soup. Yet it is not about drinking soup daily. It's about drinking different soups according to the different weather changes in the four seasons. For example, in spring and summer, you should drink soups that remove dampness. Autumn and winter climates are relatively dry, so you should drink moisturizing soup, usually with meals.

HOW POPULAR ARE CHINESE HERBAL SOUPS IN ASIA? HOW DO THE CHINESE FEEL ABOUT THIS SOUP CULTURE THEMSELVES?

Not every country in Asia drinks herbal soup. Because Chinese people pay more attention to herbal soups, places with a larger Chinese population have this practice of drinking soups. Generally Chinese people think that herbal soup is one of the methods of health preservation, which can regulate the body, prevent illnesses, and treat disease.

ARE HERBAL SOUPS CONSIDERED MEDICINE?

Since ancient times, Chinese medicine has had the theory that "medicine and food share the same source" (also called "the same source for treatment of illnesses and food"). This theory holds that many foods are both food and medicine, and food and medicine can also prevent and treat diseases. In ancient primitive societies, people discovered the taste and efficacy of various foods and medicines in the process of searching for food. They realized that many foods can be used for medicine and many medicines can also be eaten. It is difficult to distinguish strictly between the two. This is the basis of the "medicine and food homology" theory and the basis of diet therapy, now known as culinary medicine.

DO ANY OF THE HERBS IN THE SOUPS HAVE SIDE EFFECTS OR CAUSE ALLERGIC REACTIONS?

The soup that Chinese people usually drink is a combination of ingredients and medicinal materials. The medicinal materials used are relatively mild, called *shangyao* (literally meaning "high-grade medicine") in medical books, and have fewer side effects. Chinese people have been accustomed to it for thousands of years. There is no major harmful effect, so the side effects or allergic reactions caused by the soup are relatively small. If the medicine used in the soup involves medicinal herbs that are rarely used for human consumption or the quantity of medicine used is excessive, then it may cause side effects or cause allergies.

The use of Traditional Chinese Medicine emphasizes the prescription of the right medicine, reasonable compatibility, plus the appropriate dosage, and the correct decoction method. Even very mild Chinese medicine may produce adverse reactions and cause side effects if the dose is too large. Traditional Chinese Medicine contains complex chemical components. Due to differences in personal physique, the components contained in some Chinese medicines can also cause sensitive reactions. If you have side effects, like vomiting and dizziness or allergies after taking Chinese medicine, it is probably wrong for you. You should stop taking it immediately and inform your doctor at the same time.

ARE ALL CHINESE HERBS IMPORTED FROM CHINA? WHAT ARE THEIR STANDARDS FOR PROCESSING THERE?

Most Chinese herbal medicines in America are imported from China. China now has stricter regulations on Chinese herbal medicines than ever before. There are also pharmacopoeia guidelines on the amount and combination of medicinal herbs.

WILL THESE SOUPS INTERFERE WITH THE WESTERN MEDICINE PEOPLE TAKE?

Generally the medicinal materials and ingredients used in these soups are relatively mild, so they seldom interfere with Western medicines, such as medicines for diabetes and blood pressure. Chinese medicine practitioners generally advise patients that if they need to take Western medicines, it is best to take Chinese decoctions or any food involving Chinese medicinal herbs two hours before or after the dose.

WHY DO PEOPLE DEVALUE HERBAL MEDICINE? WHY IS IT REJECTED IN THE WESTERN WORLD?

Most people look down on Chinese medicine because they do not know or understand it. The culture of Chinese medicine is based on the ancient theory of yin and yang and the five elements. Even many Chinese people don't really understand the theory. Some people even think Chinese medicine is superstition. So if even Chinese don't understand Chinese medicine thoroughly, how could Westerners with different languages and cultures?

CAN PEOPLE CHANGE FROM A COLD BODY TYPE TO A HOT BODY TYPE OVER TIME?

A person's physique changes with time, environment, lifestyle conditioning, and other factors. Regardless of whether a cold body type becomes a hot body type, a hot body type turns cold, or the deficiency disappears, these changes can occur because of our lifestyle, such as diet and exercise and our environment, and sometimes due to immigration or climate change. Including therapy soups in our diet, such as dehumidification soups, heat clearing soups, or warm yang-boosting soups, may slowly change your body type after a long period of conditioning.

WHAT IS THE CHANCE OF FAILURE IN COOKING THESE SOUPS?

These soups are usually based on a combination of dietary therapy and medicinal herbs. The time and heat (slow fire, high fire) of the soup should be controlled well. However, if the wrong ingredients are used, the amount is mismatched, or the soup is cooked for too long or insufficient time, the effect of the soup will be altered.

MANY OF THE RECIPES IN THIS BOOK MAKE FOUR SERVINGS. IF SOME-BODY LIVES ALONE, CAN THAT PERSON ADJUST THE SIZES IN THE INGREDIENTS FOR ONE PORTION?

Generally soups and diets are calculated based on four people. If only one person drinks it, the serving size can be reduced by dividing by four. You can reduce the amount according to your needs. Or you can drink the same soup over two days without having to reduce the serving size too much.

CAN PEOPLE BOIL A SOUP, PUT IT IN THE REFRIGERATOR, AND THEN DRINK IT OVER A FEW DAYS? ARE THERE EXPIRATION DATES ON SOUPS?

If there is leftover soup, it can be stored in the refrigerator for no more than two days. It is best to store the strained broth and the residue ingredients separately. You can also just store the broth and throw away the ingredients.

CAN PEOPLE DRINK THE SOUPS COLD WITHOUT HEATING THEM UP?

If you are a hot body type or not into eating hot food, you can drink the soup at room temperature. However, if the soup is kept in the refrigerator, it is best to boil it again so you do not drink cold soup.

HOW DO APRICOT KERNELS DIFFER FROM ALMONDS? THEY TASTE VERY SIMILAR.

Although both sweet apricot kernels (also known as southern almonds in Chinese) and bitter apricot kernels (also known as northern almonds in Chinese) are known as "almonds" in Chinese, there is a big difference in their tastes and medicinal effects. The sweet apricot kernels are used mainly for food, and the bitter apricot kernels are used as medicinal herbs. The bitter apricot kernels have a small amount of toxins and cannot be eaten raw.

Sweet apricot kernels are sweeter. They have the effect of moisturizing the body and nourishing the lungs and skin and can cure a cough, asthma, dry intestines, and constipation. Bitter apricot kernels have a bitter taste. They are mild in nature, can relieve a cough and asthma, moisten the intestines, and relax bowel movements. They can be used in combination with sweet apricot kernels to moisturize the lungs better.

MOST OF THE SOUPS USE PORK AS A SOURCE OF MEAT. WHY IS THIS?

Pork is neutral in nature, both sweet and salty. It has the effects of tonifying deficiency, moisturizing and supplementing yin energy, and nourishing blood. From the perspective of TCM, it is suitable for cooking soup, especially for people with yin deficiency or anemia, or suffering from malnutrition. Of course, people with healthy physiques reap the same benefits.

IF SOMEBODY DOES NOT EAT PORK, WHAT OTHER MEAT CAN BE SUB-STITUTED IN THE RECIPES?

You can use chicken instead. Women with weak physiques sometimes can use black bone chicken instead of regular chicken in winter soups. Otherwise, regular chicken is fine for cooking soup for the entire family. You can also use pigeon or teal to make soup. If you don't want to use meat at all, you can use dried scallops instead.

DO THESE SOUPS FIT EVERY GEOGRAPHICAL AREA WITH VARIATION OF TEMPERATURE IN SEASONS?

Differences in regions and climate change make people's physiques different. Traditional Chinese medicine practitioners focus on adapting to local conditions. Because the geographical environment is different in various aspects, the medicines and ingredients used will be different. For example, northern China is relatively dry, so northerners tolerate stronger medicinal materials, while the South is relatively humid, so something like yarrow is not as suitable for southerners. Another point is that people's physique changes, so that will affect the type of soup best for them.

HOW DO YOU COMPARE THESE HERBAL SOUPS WITH WESTERN SOUPS?

Chinese medicine soups are tailored to the physique of each person, and the requirements of adapting measures to the time and adapting to local conditions are added. The soup is made with suitable medicinal materials, and medicines are used to satisfy different needs. For example, an initial illness can be treated with diet therapy or culinary medicine. If the effect is not achieved, then stick with just herbal medicine.

CAN PEOPLE WITH DIABETES DRINK THESE SOUPS?

People with diabetes can drink these soups as long as they avoid sweet and overly sweetened ingredients. Alternatives can be used. For example, monk fruit is a natural sweetener. Adding a small amount when boiling soup will not affect someone who has diabetes.

HOW DO HERBAL MEDICINES, TCM, AND AYURVEDIC MEDICINE DIFFER?

The ancient Indian medical system, also known as Ayurveda, is based on ancient writings that rely on "natural" and holistic methods to achieve physical and mental health. Ayurvedic medicine is one of the oldest medical systems in the world and is still one of India's traditional health care systems. Ayurvedic therapy combines products (mainly from plants, but may also include animals, metals, and minerals), diet, exercise, and lifestyle.

Ayurveda, traditional Indian medicine, and traditional Chinese medicine are the oldest existing traditional medicines. Global interest in traditional medicine is increasing. The monitoring and standardization of herbal and traditional medicine is underway. China has successfully promoted the development of its treatments through research and science-based methods, while Ayurveda in India still needs broader scientific research and a stronger evidence base. These great traditions need to be resolved in order to compete in the global market of medical treatment.

Traditional Chinese medicine focuses on the balance of body and mind, while Ayurveda covers body and mind, spirit, and connection with the higher self to achieve higher consciousness.

IS IT SAFE TO PURCHASE CHINESE HERBS ONLINE?

To buy Chinese herbs, choose a reliable supplier. Of course, it is best to buy at a physical Chinese herbal store, where you can see the quality of the herbs. If you must purchase online, it is best to choose a supplier with a good reputation and after-sales service, such as a contact number, preferably an address. Then after receiving the Chinese herbs through the mail, if you have any questions, you can at least contact the supplier for further questions.

WHEN PICKING A TCM PRACTITIONER, WHAT SHOULD PEOPLE LOOK FOR?

It is important to choose TCM physicians who are formally registered or licensed in the local area. You need to research their experience, education, and background to make sure they are well qualified. In addition to medical skills, Chinese medicine practitioners must also have medical ethics. There is a saying in Chinese medicine that "a great doctor is also honest and sincere," which means that regardless of whether the patient is poor or rich, family or a stranger, he or she will treat the patient with all his or her heart. Also, an elderly Chinese medicine doctor usually accumulates more clinical experience. You should always base your selection of a doctor on reputation and recommendations by multiple acquaintances and friends.

WHAT ARE TCM'S STRENGTHS?

Traditional Chinese medicine treats patients according to the nature of the illness, whether it is long term or short term, acute or chronic. It is especially good at treating chronic diseases such as diabetes. Chinese medicine prescribes specially formulated medicines according to the different stages and physical changes of patients and also advises patients to drink conditioning soups. For example, diabetes is a form of yin deficiency, so it is recommended to drink nourishing yin soups, with herbs such as adenophora or polygonatum. In addition, from the perspective of Western medicine, diabetes is caused by insulin problems. In TCM, the pancreas (which regulates insulin) belongs to the spleen. Thus, it is recommended to drink more herbal soups that can strengthen and benefit the spleen.

CAN YOU SHARE A STORY ABOUT AN HERBAL SOUP THAT IS EFFECTIVE FOR A CERTAIN ILLNESS THAT YOU PERSONALLY HAVE EXPERIENCE WITH?

There is a real-life example of a clinical trial on an herbal soup that I have participated in. Many years ago, when I was the deputy director of the Macau Institute for Applied Research in Medicine and Health, I came into contact with a family's secret recipe, a soup using two main Chinese medicinal materials: chicken feces vine and pork soup with raw coix seeds. This soup seemed to be effective in controlling diabetes and could reduce glycosylated hemoglobin (HbA1c). For patients who had been consuming the soup or a tea that we made the formula into [the English branded name is PSP, and the Chinese brand name is Yibao] for many years, we discovered that in addition to controlling their blood sugar, older patients, especially men with prostate problems who have frequent nocturia, did better. After taking PSP, nocturia was also significantly reduced in frequency. For my patients' convenience, we have since made the formula into tablets.

INDEX

ACKNOWLEDGMENTS

For more information, visit our book's website at www.healingherbalsoups.com. The website will direct you to where to buy herbs and products that are featured in the recipes in this book.

This book was made possible with the expertise and assistance of several people who share our love of soup making and wellness.

Our eternal gratitude goes out to Christine Fahey and Jennifer Robinson for initiating our project during uncertain times.

A big thank-you to Dr. Shiu Hon Chui, Elaine Leung, Yao Qin Wu, Dylan Ho, Jeni Afuso, Marianne Kai, Brendan Minto, Lan Ong, and the entire Wing Hop Fung family for their direct contributions to the book.

We would not be here without the guidance of our manager, Mike Vanderhei, and our literary agents Anna Petkovich, Celeste Fine, and Steven Fisher.

Thank you to our entire team at Tiller Press and Simon & Schuster: Theresa DiMasi, Anja Schmidt, Michael Andersen, Matthew Ryan, Patrick Sullivan, Jennifer Chung, Samantha Lubash, Ian King, Beverly Miller, Laura Flavin, and Lauren Ollerhead.

And finally, a big shout-out to all of you who bought this book. May the recipes bring you delicious experiences and good health for years to come.

ABOUT THE AUTHORS

Rose Cheung is a mother and entrepreneur. She inherited her fondness for soup from her mother, who raised her in a traditional Chinese family in Hong Kong. After Rose moved to the United States to attend college, she got married and settled down in Southern California. She and her husband opened and owned a Chinese restaurant in Hermosa Beach for four years.

As a full-time working mother raising two young daughters, Rose continued the Cantonese custom of making soup and two dishes for every meal. She faced all the challenges of bringing up children—she watched them catch colds and coughs from school and whenever the weather changed.

Rose began to realize that maintenance was just as important as the cure. She started studying old world soup recipes from China in hopes of building her daughters' immune systems. There is an old Chinese saying that you first use food to cure yourself and then drugs later, only if the first option is not effective.

Rose became involved with Chinese herbs when her mother was diagnosed with lymphoma. She tried all possible ways to make her mother live longer than expected. Because of Rose's interactions with some of the best Chinese herbalists in Los Angeles and China, her curiosity also led her to learn a lot about what was best not only for her mother but for the human body generally. In addition, she learned how food can supplement and support a patient's health and make treatment more effective.

Rose's passion for Chinese medicine, food, and herbs has grown so much that in 2009, she sponsored the development of an herbal formula used to treat diabetes at the Macau University of Science and Technology. The product was subsequently patented and is currently available through select traditional Chinese Medicine clinics in Asia.

☼

Genevieve Wong is a four-time Emmy-nominated producer and writer. As a journalist, she has reported for *NBC News*, the *New York Post*, the *Los Angeles Times*, and other news organizations. She is also a former cooking producer for *The Nate Show*, where she worked alongside Todd English, Bobby Flay, and other celebrity chefs.

After two decades of suffering from conditions like eczema, allergies, and asthma, Genevieve became extremely interested in TCM at the age of twenty-three and, by default, began to learn about the healing powers of Chinese herbal soups. Although she does not consider herself to be a domestic person, it is not unusual to find Genevieve in the kitchen, fanning the flames of her herbal concoctions or boiling healing herbal soups and porridges for her friends and family who are sick or pregnant.